Walk This Way

'This book invites us to leave the stressful rat race of our daily lives and to journey back in time with a few of those who had a special friendship with Jesus. Here is an opportunity to travel with Brother Lawrence, St Teresa of Avila and St Benedict to learn vital spiritual practices for our busy lives that will enable us to also walk more closely to the One who calls us to that quiet centre. A must for all those who want learn a spirituality that draws us into the deep ways.'

TOM SINE, Mustard Seed Associates

'Rook and Holmes team up to offer us more than an academic exercise of discipleship, more than sweet rhetoric of faith – they offer an invitation, from the Word Himself to take the whole trip! A lifelong journey with Jesus begins with "follow me" and culminates with the fullness of God's Kingdom on earth. Make the trip – don't miss out on the depths or heights of life abundant. Stop contemplating discipleship – pick up the book – give it a read and then live it out!'

**DANIELLE STRICKLAND, Social Justice Director,
The Salvation Army (Australia Southern Territory)**

'A companion and introduction to the wisdom and treasures of those who have travelled the road of following Christ before us and whose insights can illumine our journeys of faith for today.'

**ROY SEARLE, Leader, Northumbria Community
and former President of the Baptist Union of Great Britain**

'Disciples of Jesus Christ need to know the riches of the spiritual tradition we inherit. These extracts – modern re-workings of some of the great spiritual classics – will nourish the soul, provoke the mind, and maybe even send us back to read Bunyan, Herbert and St Theresa in the original versions.'

PETE BROADBENT, Bishop of Willesden

'For two millennia men and women have apprenticed themselves to Christ. Those of us who are wise will listen to, and learn from, their experience as they call us to *Walk This Way*. In doing so, we will find that we are better equipped to meet the challenges of life and following Christ today.'

STEVE CHALKE, Founder of Oasis Global and Faithworks

'Francis of Assisi urged the brothers who journeyed with him to "follow in the footsteps of Christ". By rewriting their work in contemporary language, *Walk This Way* makes accessible the wisdom of many who have heeded the friar's advice and allows us to enter into their pilgrimages of faith. If you ever feel like you are walking alone then here's an opportunity to learn from the many that have walked this way before and see how their paths offer hope and fresh possibilities for 21st century followers.'

ANDREW GRINNELL, Emerging Missions Officer for The Salvation Army

Walk This Way

On the road with Jesus

Edited by
STEPHEN R. HOLMES and RUSSELL ROOK

MILTON KEYNES ● COLORADO SPRINGS ● HYDERABAD

Copyright © 2009 Stephen R. Holmes and Russell Rook

15 14 13 12 11 10 09   7 6 5 4 3 2 1

First published 2009 by Paternoster
Paternoster is an imprint of Authentic Media
9 Holdom Avenue, Bletchley, Milton Keynes, Bucks, MK1 1QR, UK
1820 Jet Stream Drive, Colorado Springs, CO 80921, USA
Medchal Road, Jeedimetla Village, Secunderabad 500 055, A.P., India
www.authenticmedia.co.uk

Authentic Media is a division of IBS-STL U.K., limited by guarantee,
with its Registered Office at Kingstown Broadway, Carlisle, Cumbria CA3 0HA.
Registered in England & Wales No. 1216232. Registered charity 270162

The right of Stephen R. Holmes and Russell Rook to be identified as the
Editors of this Work has been asserted by him in accordance with the
Copyright, Designs and Patents Act 1988.

British Library Cataloguing in Publication Data
A catalogue record for this book is available from the British Library

ISBN-13: 978-1-84227-640-2

Design by James Kessell for Scratch the Sky Ltd (www.scratchthesky.com)
Print Management by Adare
Typeset by Waverley Typesetters, Fakenham
Printed and bound in Great Britain by Bell & Bain Ltd, Glasgow

Contents

Preface

I am not a supporter of Liverpool Football Club. In fact, as a follower of their fiercest rivals I could hardly be less of a fan. That said, I'll let you into a secret. Every so often, I wish I was. It's not the history of the club, their style of play or the passion of the fans that makes me feel that way. It's just their song ...

> When you walk through a storm, Hold your head up high and don't be afraid of the dark.... You'll never walk alone! You'll never walk alone!

For all the uncouthness associated with football supporters, witnessing 40,000 fans bellowing these words with hands aloft does something for the soul. And it's not just the obvious that moves me. For while the hymn-like tenor and worshipful posture of the singers reminds us that we are all – no matter how unbelieving or religiously disinterested – worshipful creatures, the song also rings true for God's people, the church. The reason why the church works, why Christian discipleship offers life to the full and why following Jesus is possible in the first place is because we don't have to do it alone. If as Father, Son and Spirit the creator doesn't walk alone, it seems unsurprising that we, his creatures, find solitary confinement and loneliness unattractive. As one of my friends is fond of pointing out, 'There really are no lone rangers in this life. Even the original Lone Ranger wasn't really alone. After all, he had his horse *and* Tonto!'

Since the very first of their number was called, disciples have never had to walk alone. Discipleship by its very nature is a journey with Jesus. In pursuit of his kingdom we travel through the dusty dailyness in his company. Like Cleopas and his companion on the road to Emmaus, there are days when we don't even know he is there. On others his proximity is palpable. Whether visible or invisible, he remains as good as his word and is present among us till the end of the age. With the resurrected Jesus as our teacher and rabbi we'll never walk alone.

The communal nature of discipleship doesn't stop with Christ. A friend of mine, Brian, has a thing about Carolyn Joyce Carty's poem, *Footprints*. For anyone who has not come across this poem, it allegorises the Christian life as a long walk along a sandy road. Having travelled many miles, the traveller turns to review on the journey so far only to observe two sets of footprints along life's way. Upon reflection she observes that the second pair of footprints can only be those of Christ her ever present companion. And yet, in what were the harder parts of the journey there appears to be only one set of prints. No sooner has she contemplated the possibility that Christ left her to walk this path alone than she is reassured that the lone prints are due to the fact that Christ had carried her over this most testing terrain.

While not wanting to glibly denigrate what is a meaningful piece of poetry for Christians around the world, Brian fights the urge not to prophetically combust every time he sees a tea towel, poster or bookmark with said stanzas on it. Brian's problem is the last part of the poem. You see as with many of us, when Brian looks back on life's most testing times he doesn't see one pair of footprints but many. It is then that he is reminded that Christ carried him through that time with the help of his people, the church.

As we walk with Jesus through the difficulties of day-to-day living, not to mention the challenge of following him, we never walk alone. Along life's way we are joined by countless brothers and sisters who share our hopes and dreams, pains and frustrations. Membership of the church provides us with many fellow travellers with whom to share the highs and lows of life on the road. What's more, we're not simply accompanied by present-day disciples. Countless others have trodden this path before and provide expert maps and guides for us to use along the way. Remembering and revising the lessons that Christ taught them provides us with profound teaching for our own time. With this in mind we present to you *Walk This Way*, a collection of writings all of which are simultaneously historic and modern.

The following forty extracts were compiled for your encouragement, inspiration and learning. By reading these classic Christian texts and teachings we hope that you'll discover anew Christ's presence and leading in your own life. As you dip into the lives and works of these Christian saints, we desire that Jesus will lead you deeper into truth. Above all we pray that, through the words and experience of his people, you'll know the presence and guidance of the greatest teacher who ever lived. For this way you won't have to walk alone.

There is an obvious danger in trying to contemporize historic documents and ancient sources. While hoping to bring the content to life there is also a risk of adding to, amending or detracting from the author's original intention. However this is surely a risk worth taking in the hope that these texts can reach and affect a new audience and serve another generation.

By translating and paraphrasing this literature into contemporary English we want to fuel two necessary journeys. Recently, it has become too easy to divorce the art of spiritual formation from theological reflection. And yet, as our writers and speakers constantly remind us, it is impossible to have one without the other. It is no good for the more spiritual among us to eschew theological learning for more practical devotions. Likewise the learned will never understand theology if they do not engage their hearts and prayers as well as their brains and their books. Jesus calls all disciples to enjoy a richer spirituality through a deeper knowledge of his Father and visa versa. We pray that the disciples who read these passages will hear Christ's call both loud and clear.

The inspiration for this book came from the fine work undertaken in the development of a theme for *Spring Harvest* 2009. Taking the title *Apprentice: Walking in the Way of Christ*, Spring Harvest has provided tens of thousands of Christians with the opportunity to explore and extend their walk with Jesus. We are indebted in particular to Steve Chalke, who has initiated and overseen the development of the theme. In addition, we are hugely grateful to the many members of the Spring Harvest team for all they have done to equip the church for action. We hope that *Walk This Way* will provide a valuable resource for those travelling on from this life-changing event.

As ever, Robin Parry at Paternoster has provided essential expertise and support. As a publisher, Robin's commitment to putting titles into print, books onto shelves and change into the church is inspirational. Our thanks go to him and the staff at Paternoster and Authentic. We are also grateful to Andrew Grinnell for his input into our earliest discussions; it is a different book from the one Andrew helped us imagine, but it would not be what it is without his thoughts.

Finally, and most of all, our thanks go to Matt Little who has spent more hours than we can count searching and reading, accepting and rejecting, and cutting and pasting classic Christian texts for inclusion in this book. His help in sourcing extracts, developing ideas and preparing the final manuscript has made all of this possible. What's more, his Christlike spirit and passion for discipleship demonstrates what this book is all about.

As you read the passages ahead and join those who have walked this way before, our single hope and greatest prayer is that you will come to see and hear Jesus as he walks beside you. As you walk this way may you also know that you'll never walk alone!

RUSSELL ROOK
London
September 2008

Introduction –
Spirituality for the Rest of Us

'Spirituality' is a modern and cold word for an ancient and warm idea. It describes the attempt to create harmony between our hearts and our lives, to align our convictions with our practices, to become people who say what we do and do what we say. It describes the search for integrity, for a coherent life.

Our lives are not coherent. This morning, I drove the three miles to work because it was raining and then, before starting work, responded to a Tearfund campaign by firing off an email protesting about how little the government is doing to prevent climate change. I lecture my daughters about doing things that are wrong, then do the same things myself a few minutes later. I feel the hypocrisy of every sermon I preach – how little I live it. And as for this, writing a book about prayer ... There is some comfort in knowing that I am not alone in this; it is general human experience. We know the good, and do not do it. We know what is wrong, and we do that instead.

The Christian account of the world paints the problem in bold and vivid colours: as fallen, sinful people, our hearts and hands are strangely out of step. We do the things we don't want to do, and don't do the things we do want to do, as Paul puts it in Romans 7. We can look with longing, it is true, to a place where this was not the case – a state of original righteousness when God created all things good and Adam and Eve could stand before him concealing nothing and unashamed. But that reality is lost to us now; sin warps and distorts every human life. We are unintegrated, incoherent – fallen.

In Jesus, we have the promise of new creation, the re-integration of our lives. Jesus, alone among the children of Eve, lived with integrity, a coherent life. The chaos and disorder of sin assailed him, but could not overcome him. Through the cross and resurrection, he re-ordered the world, decisively ending the spread of sin and chaos. The shining promise is that the day will come when Jesus will return and renew the world – and us with it. As we live in faithful hope of that coming, God has graciously given us his Holy Spirit, so we can know the firstfruits of that new creation (Rom. 8:23). And so now, day by day, we are being remade – renewed into people whose lives are coherent as Jesus' life was. This, in Christian terms, is spirituality. I say 'in Christian terms' because others try to find integrity and coherence in other ways. Some will strive to re-create their own lives; others will commit themselves to practices of meditation or yoga or similar disciplines. God is gracious to all, and it seems to me that the general experience of people who are seriously trying to improve themselves in such ways is that they attain a measure of success. But the truth as it is given in Scripture, and as we know it in our own lives if we are honest, is that our disorder, our dis-integration, our sin is far, far more radical than that. We need to be re-created from without, to be raised from death and decay to life and hope.

This renewal is the work of the Holy Spirit, of course, but God gives us ways to place ourselves in the hands of the Spirit, to make ourselves available for renewal. Our task is to be easy clay for the potter to shape, if you like. God works on us, but we can turn ourselves so that God's work runs with, not against, the grain of our lives. 'Christian spirituality' is just what we do to do this. It is about regular prayer and Bible reading, and about disciplines of fasting, giving and the like. As these become more and more a part of our life, we start to live in a place where we are open to the Spirit's work and available for God's leading. And God starts to put us back together, so that our lives increasingly reflect the holiness, the wholeness, the integrity that God calls us to, and offers to us in Jesus. Christian spirituality is about becoming human again – really human, the way Jesus was human.

The struggle to pray

If Christian spirituality is about becoming human again, why is it something so many of us find hard?

I had been preaching regularly for several years before I preached my first sermon on prayer. This wasn't because I thought prayer didn't matter; I knew, of course, that it was vital – more vital than almost anything else. I also knew, however, that everyone I met in church felt guilty about their prayer life, and guilt is no way to motivate people (it might work – although I doubt it – but it is a million miles from the gospel of Jesus Christ). And I knew that almost every talk I had ever heard on prayer just left people feeling even more guilty. Speakers and preachers seemed to assume that people didn't want to pray, and needed to be told that they ought to want to. The problem, they said, was a lack of desire, a lack of understanding of the importance of prayer (and personal Bible reading too).

The people I knew, however, wanted to have a satisfying prayer life. They knew it was important; that was why they felt guilty about it. Someone giving them even more reasons why it was important just made them feel more guilty. It was a bit like telling someone who is seriously overweight that there are all sorts of lifestyle and health and self-esteem reasons why they would be so much better off if they were thin and muscular. They know that – what they need is to see a route from here to there that they can imagine themselves walking. Most of the Christians I have talked to about prayer have a picture in their heads of what a good prayer life would look like, but they have no idea how to get there, or they have tried, and given up discouraged, when the road turned out to be so hard.

I remember, sitting one Friday afternoon in the library of the college where I was teaching, reading a book I wanted to use for a course, when suddenly a truth I sort of knew coalesced into a sentence in my head: 'prayer is a gift God gives, not a duty God commands'. I realized that I could preach this, and that Sunday evening I did.

It wasn't, in technical terms, a very good sermon. The balance of the construction was wrong; it was a bit ragged around the edges. I've preached it six or seven times since, and still not got it right. Every time I preach that message, however, I get fantastic reactions. I just try to tell people that prayer is not some clever technique that they are bad at and God wants them to be good at; it is a wonderful gift that he gives to us to welcome us into the glorious light and warmth of his transforming love. We do not need to live up to any model of prayer that others have told us is right because it works for them, any more than I need to live up to any model of being a husband that someone else has worked out. Instead, just as I need to find ways of loving and honouring Heather that work for her and me, we need to find ways of prayer that work for us, that allow us to bask in the glow of God's love on a regular basis, and so to begin to reflect that glow a little in our own lives.

Praying as you can

The best piece of advice on prayer I ever heard was this: 'Pray as you can, not as you can't.' It was given to me by a slightly mad charismatic Catholic nun many years ago. It was not original to her; John Chapman, the Abbot of Downside Abbey in the 1930s, first said it. The point is this: too many of us have a model of what 'proper' prayer looks like in our heads. And we don't live up to that model, so we rapidly give up on praying. We find we cannot know God's love one way, and we've been told it's the right way, so we end up trying to be content with far-off glimpses, trying to believe what others tell us about God.

God doesn't want us to know his love second-hand, or from fleeting glimpses. In Psalm 63, David recalls what it is to know God, and compares it to rich and satisfying food. If our experience of God is not like that, we are missing out on something God has given us. It seems to me that most of us are missing out. There was a story in the papers about twenty years ago about an elderly woman who had died in Chicago. She'd been living in a tiny apartment, strictly rationing how often she had the heating on, buying not quite enough food – a classic story of elderly poverty. Her next-of-kin inherited millions of dollars. She had worked in youth as a housekeeper for a rich industrialist, who had made her a gift of stocks and shares, and he had chosen well. She didn't know what they were, however, and so kept them in a box under her bed, living as if she had almost nothing. Too many Christians I know live as if they have almost nothing, because they don't know what to do with the wonderful gift that God has given them in Christ.

Part of the problem, I think, is that we have very set expectations of what will work and what won't. There are 'proper' ways of maintaining a spiritual life, and if they don't work for you or me, the problem is with us (we need to try harder!) not with the method. This is what seems wrong-headed to me. There are no proper ways of loving someone, no formulas that will shape a strong relationship for every single couple. People are just too different for that. This week I talked with a senior Christian leader, who held a national role in his denomination, who had lived on a different continent from his wife for two years recently. It was the life God had called them to, and he bore profound, if surprised, testimony to the renewal of their individual lives and of their relationship that it had brought about. For them, it worked. For thousands of others, it would not. There are no proper ways of living a loving relationship, nothing beyond the continuing command to discover in humility and constant repentance what love looks like here and now, in our particular situation. When we talk about our relationship with God, God does not change of course, but people are still just too different for any one way of experiencing, enjoying, and being transformed by God's love to work well for us all, at every point in our lives.

I think of friends who were taught a very particular pattern of prayer and Bible study when they were students. When we were students it worked, for at least some of us; this pattern fitted the shape of our lives. The subtle message that came out, however, was that the *real* Christian prays and reads the Bible for at least twenty minutes before breakfast every single morning. Well, perhaps – but it's not a pattern I can find in the Bible (praying all night is far more common there), and it's not one that makes any sense for people with young families (at least young families who wake at the sort of hours ours do . . .). You can make it work, force yourself to do it by ignoring the children and a great effort of willpower, but why make life more difficult than it needs to be?

And it happens when Christians get together, too. I really don't like prayer meetings. For me, they happen too fast. When I pray, I find I need a little time to quieten down, to relax, to become aware of God's presence; then I can begin to bring things before God meaningfully. In a traditional prayer meeting, each time someone else prays, I find I need a minute or two to process that before I'm ready to pray – by that time someone else has started, and so it goes.

I was once on a group retreat with a group of people I knew well. The leader called us all back together and asked what God had been saying to us; one after another of my friends spoke of clear and powerful revelations from God, that helped them directly with issues they were facing in their lives or churches (we were all young church leaders). As the next session started, I went off into the chapel and spent some time telling God exactly what I thought of his rather-too-familiar silence in my own life. Then I picked up a pen and started writing . . .

. . . I still have that piece of paper. It contains a revelation, perhaps, but certainly a realization that God's calling on my life would involve my learning to live with questions, to worry away at them, to find answers by thinking hard, and that it would be through that worrying and wrestling that I would be, by God's grace, of some use to the church and in the world. And if that was going to be my life, then it implied certain things about what my experience of prayer was going to be like. I realized then that I should not look for spectacular revelations in response to my prayers, at least not very often. That would go against the life and ministry God has called me to, damage the things God has given me to do. Pray as you can, not as you can't.

Finding the right shoes to pray in

It is not news to announce that we are all different: we think in different ways, we learn in different ways. God has given us different gifts and different callings. Our brains are wired differently. More than that, we live different lives with different work, family and other commitments. God has put us in different places.

Because of this – because of the way God has made us, and the way God has led us – we cannot operate with a 'one size fits all' spirituality. There is no one right way of doing things that will suit everyone. Or, rather, we *can* operate with a 'one size fits all' spirituality, but it actually won't fit most of us. In many different ways, it will rub against some of us, or be too loose for others.

Where I need a bit of space, it will be tight and constricting; where you need a bit of support, it will be floppy and useless. And so the structure will actually hinder our growth in godliness, rather than help it.

Earlier this year, I bought my first pair of proper running shoes. I'd tried running regularly from time to time before, in whatever pair of cheap trainers I happened to own, but I'd always given up fairly quickly, because one of my ankles started to hurt. But this time I wanted to make it work, so I summoned up the courage to go into the running shop in town. As I walked in I felt slightly heartened: the man behind the counter was more overweight than I am. He knew something about running shoes though. He soon had my shoes and socks off and my trousers rolled up, and just as I was wondering if I'd said some secret code-word by accident, and this was a strange freemasons' ritual, he lay on the floor in front of me and told me to walk away from him. This did nothing to calm my suspicions. After five steps he jumped up, told me which ankle normally hurt and where, and that it was all because I suffered from 'serious over-pronation', which I thought sounded terminal, but apparently can be cured by just wearing the right shoes. So he grabbed a pair of shoes from the display, put them on me, then he went and lay down on the pavement while I ran past him. I won't say those shoes are perfect – apart from anything else, they are a really bright blue, which isn't me at all – but they are right for me. They give me the support I need where I need it, so that my ankle stays healthy, and I can feel the bounce and spring in them. They help me to run, and to keep on running. Now I just need to find someone who can sell me a house that isn't on a steep hill, and some dry, sunny weather, and I'll be there in the marathon …

I have come to realize that the ways I was taught to pray and study the Bible as a young Christian were like my old trainers: they weren't bad, and they worked for everyone after a fashion, but when things got high intensity, like a few miles of road running, for me they weren't up to the job. I need something different, something that is just right for me, rather than OK for everyone. And what works for me will not work for many other people – just like someone with a different running style would probably be hampered or even injured by my shoes – but that is fine, so long as we can all find something that fits us.

Christian retreat houses and spiritual directors (a frightening term for people God has called and gifted to help others to learn to pray) have known this for a while – probably more or less forever, actually, just as athletes have known that some shoes work for them and that some don't (for as long as they have been wearing shoes). But like running shoes, in recent years they have started to develop systems for spotting people's needs and helping them. If you look over the programme of a retreat centre these days, you are very likely to find, at least a few times a year, courses based around the 'Myers-Briggs Type Indicator' (MBTI), or the 'Enneagram'. These are tools to help people to understand who they are, and what works for them. They are tools to help us to discover ways of praying – and of living – that will work for us.

One of my fellow-leaders at a previous church was a clinical psychologist, and she encouraged us to explore a tool like this. It told me, among other things, that on a spectrum from 'extrovert' to 'introvert' I was right over at the introvert side. This surprised me at first as then, like now, I spent half my life on my feet talking to groups of people in lectures or sermons. Anne explained to me, however, that the scale was about comfort and energy: it's not that we introverts *can't* function in big groups, but it costs us something to do it. That made sense to me: I can turn it on in a group, but it takes something out of me; when I am tired or run down, I want to be on my own, or with one or two of a very small number of close friends. My wife jokes that there is a certain time of the evening at a party when I turn into a pumpkin, and retire into a corner alone. This also helped me understand why I have the problems I do with prayer meetings: I just don't function particularly well in a group, and so I find it hard to be spontaneous.

Other parts of the MBTI try to assess whether your natural mode is thinking or feeling, sensing or intuitive, and so on. These scales are not hard results of brain science, of course; they are just ways that might help people to understand a little better who they are and how they work, so that they can find helpful ways of praying and living. For me, the spiritual high points are when I can be alone and silent before God. I book days in monasteries or retreat centres from time to time, but I never sign up for a course or a group; that's not who I am, not what works for me. For someone else, the group will be vital, and spending time alone will drain them, make then uncomfortable, and so make it harder for them to spend serious time with God. Pray as you can, not as you can't.

Times and places

What about the timing of our prayer life? I remember well when I first realized something that should have been obvious. I was reading about the old Church of England practices of daily prayer, which happened every morning and evening. When I was at university, the college chapel followed some of this pattern, and held daily prayers, a brief ten minutes before dinner every evening. At the time I found it enormously helpful, hearing the Scriptures read and repeating familiar words of worship and prayer every day. A few years later, I read a discussion of the timing of the prayers, which pointed out that they were designed to fit around the daily rhythms of agricultural work. It suddenly struck me: most of my regular rhythms were weekly, not daily. I do not have to milk the cows at the same time every morning – but I do have a set of daytime and evening commitments that come around in the same slot each week – and I suppose that this is very common in our culture today. Early Monday evening the children go to swimming lessons; Wednesday night is home group; Thursday morning the big team meeting at work that needs preparation and sets agendas for the rest of the week; many things seem to happen on a weekly basis.

The old Anglican pattern of prayer worked with the lives of the people it was designed for, enabling prayer and life to fit easily together. Perhaps for some of us a weekly pattern, rather than a daily pattern, would do the same thing today? Or we might try to find a pattern that recognizes the differences between weekdays and weekends, if that is the structure of our lives. The point is doing what the *Book of Common Prayer* tried to do: finding a way of prayer that fits with the necessary rhythms of our lives.

I can already hear in my head the voice of my well-meaning and earnest university Christian Union leader: 'your quiet time should come first – make the rest of your life fit around it!' But why? God called me to the work I am doing, and called Heather to her profession too; God chose to give us the precious gift of children; family and professional commitments are not things that are in the way of my service of God, they are part of it. There is no command in Scripture that says we should pray first thing every morning (there really isn't – go and look! Psalm 119:164 suggests praying seven times a day; Daniel prayed three times a day. But once a day in the morning is just not there). Meeting with God in prayer and worship is vital to our lives, but God seems to have given us the freedom to find and set our own patterns that work for us. Pray as you can, not as you can't!

Twenty minutes a morning, seven days a week, is between two and two-and-a-half hours; take that as a target to aim for, if only for the sake of argument. Perhaps you are a single parent, with children at school during the week, but very busy weekends; could you find half an hour while the children are out each weekday? Perhaps your job now takes you away from home two nights a week, making the remaining family time precious; could you give a solid hour of prayer and Bible reading those two nights, alone in a hotel room or wherever? Maybe the way your week works there is a big gap Thursday afternoon, but the rest is pressured; why not make that a really serious time of Bible study, with briefer prayers the rest of the week? At the university where I currently teach, there is a communion service every Tuesday lunchtime during term; if you have an opportunity like this that is something that is helpful for you, why not build it in to your weekly routine?

Alternatively, perhaps the suggestions in Scripture about praying more than once a day attract you. For a while, Heather and I would pray individually in the morning and together at night. Actually, it didn't really suit either of us, but it's something we tried. These days we read Scripture and pray with our children just before they go to bed each night; that becomes one of the fixed points in the day, around which we can add others, which vary through the week. Many published aids to private prayer offer set prayers and Bible readings for both morning and evening; some also offer a lunchtime or a late evening ('compline') resource. The only question is, what works for you? What helps you to develop and maintain the life of devotion you need and want? Pray as you can, not as you can't!

I have just mentioned published resources; there are lots of them. Some of them just suggest a pattern of Scripture reading and leave you to construct your own prayers around it; others offer you a Scripture reading and some thoughts or guidelines for prayer; others again offer a briefer or fuller set liturgy, which guides most of your praying. (We have included a list of resources in the Bibliography at the end of this book.) What about set liturgies? Some people seem to find them boring and deadening; others find familiar words helpful. There isn't a right answer: try them, see if they work for you, and if they do, use them. If not, leave them for others. There are other aids, suggesting a looser structure to a time of prayer ('ACTS' is a famous one: begin by Adoring God in worship; move to Confession of sin; give Thanks for God's gifts and for answered prayers; then move to Supplication – asking God for help for yourself and others). Or you might let the Scripture passage you are reading shape your prayer (see the section on praying with the Bible later). The only point is, what works for you.

Where are you going to pray? Wherever you happen to be? In the same place each day or week? Inside? Outside? At home? At work? I knew someone once who used to take regular prayer retreats to Heathrow Airport. Sitting in the concourse, surrounded by noise and bustling humanity, he found it easy to be drawn into prayer for the people he could see, for places whose names came over the tannoy and so on. If that works for you (and you can afford an airport car park!), why not? If you lack a local airport, perhaps praying in the park, or on a bench in a shopping centre of your town would work?

Do you find it most helpful to pray alone? With your spouse/ family? With one particular friend? In a bigger group? There's nothing magical about being on your own when you pray. It is true that Jesus would withdraw to a lonely place (Lk. 5:16), but when the disciples asked him to teach them to pray, he said 'when you (plural) pray, say "Our Father …",' suggesting he expected them to pray together. Time alone is easier to arrange than time with a friend, of course, but if it suits both of you, why not?

How are you going to pray? Silently? Aloud? Whispering, shouting, or both? By singing (not recommended if you are praying in the shopping centre …)? By writing? By drawing or painting? Will you be sitting down? Kneeling? Standing? Dancing (again, probably not in the shopping centre)? Is praying while on the train, or out for a run, what works for you? (Bible study while running might be challenging, but you can get podcasts of portions of Scripture on your iPod if you really want to try it!) It might be that sitting in your bedroom quietly for twenty minutes reading Scripture and praying before breakfast every morning is what works for you – if so, that is great; there is nothing wrong with that at all. But if it doesn't work for you, don't worry – it is not the only way to pray.

It's about getting running shoes that help you to run. I kept giving up on running because I didn't have the right kit – so running hurt (in bad ways; of course running hurts in good ways if you do it right …). I said at the beginning of this introduction that I don't believe that it is a lack of desire or discipline that stops Christian people praying. The people I have talked to over the years – as a pastor; after I have preached a sermon on prayer; in Christian conferences; even my own students sometimes, when they have brought the subject up – are people who want to pray, but find it hard. It seems to me that often they find it hard because they're trying to run in the wrong shoes.

Praying with the Bible

'All Scripture,' announces 2 Timothy 3:16, 'is God-breathed and useful …' It seems to me that all the argument about this verse is misplaced: we have talked and talked about inspiration, and what it means, and most people in churches these days understand that the Bible is true. What we don't understand is what to do with it – how is Scripture 'useful'?

One of my students had to preach a few months ago on Nehemiah 3. As we chatted about it, he commented 'Of course I believe it's all true – but what do I do with it?' This text consists almost entirely of a list of people, together with a list of which bit of the walls or gates of Jerusalem they were responsible for rebuilding. No doubt we should believe that the lists are accurate, as we should with all Scripture – but how is this passage 'useful'? How does knowing that Joiada son of Paseah, and not Malkijah son of Recab, repaired the Jeshanah Gate make any difference to, well, anything at all?

I should say that you can find good answers to this question. I told this story in a public lecture not long after Chris's sermon and got some laughs, as well as a friendly complaint afterwards from someone who turned out to be the Regius Professor of Biblical Hebrew from Oxford University, and who had recently written a learned commentary on Nehemiah explaining exactly how the text was useful. His points were really good, and I could preach a great sermon on the text now, but they relied on knowing quite a lot about where the different walls and gates were. Anyone coming to Nehemiah 3 in the course of daily devotional Bible reading is going to struggle to know what to do with it. How is God speaking to me, guiding my life, building my faith, through this passage – or a hundred others like it? We need to learn to pray with the Bible.

And, again, the way we do it will depend on who we are. For some of us, buying the learned commentary and reading up about the topography of ancient Jerusalem will be just what we want to do. Study and thinking is nourishing for us. One of the things I enjoy most about writing sermons is the work of struggling with a text of Scripture, thinking hard about what it says and what it means, and about the different ways in which that might be useful and interesting for the church today. Out of study like this, I find it easy to pray, focusing on the promises and commands and examples I have found in the text, and the ways these are relevant to my life, and to the church I will be preaching to.

Other people, however, will not find this helpful. Some, in a similar intellectual vein, might find listening to really good sermons is what brings the Scriptures alive for them. There is a list of humorous 'Christian chat-up lines' doing the rounds on Facebook at the moment; one of the better ones is '35% of my iPod memory is devoted to Mark Driscoll'. There are many really good sermons podcast on the Web (and many more pretty bad ones, it has to be said …); if it works for you, gets you thinking about how to apply Scripture in your life, and praying and acting in response, why not?

Perhaps the monologue of a sermon doesn't do it for you; group discovery, talking together about the passage, sparking off each other, finding energy and insight in different perspectives and alternative views – perhaps this is how the Bible really comes alive for you. Like group prayer, it will take a bit more organizing, but if it works for you, then it is worth the effort.

This is still fairly intellectual, though. The most ancient ways of praying with the Bible engage the imagination far more. One practice, going right back to the beginnings of church history, is called *lectio divina*, Latin for 'divine reading' (perhaps 'holy reading' would be a better English term). This, again, is something I find very helpful. It works like this: first, you get ready – find the time and space, somewhere comfortable to sit, with Bible and notebook (and pen . . .) to hand, then you take a bit of time to become quiet and calm before God, so that you are ready to hear his voice, and ask him to speak to you. Then you start to read the passage, very slowly, reading each phrase or even each word again and again, all the time listening – being attentive – to God. Typically a word or a phrase will catch hold of your imagination, so you stop reading and focus on that word or phrase; you try to discern what God is wanting to say to you through it (not necessarily what it meant in the context of the passage – the focus here is on listening to God here and now, not Bible study). Respond to what you sense God saying in prayer, and then return to the passage and read further, doing the same again.

I remember how strange this sounded when I first heard about it, so here is an example. The passage I was reading was Isaiah 43:1–7; I prayed through this passage in February 2006, as part of a 'retreat in daily life' I was taking part in for Lent that year. The notes I made afterwards went like this:

(a) 'now' v. 1: struck by the sense that God might have a word for me now – at this particular point in my life. Asked for such a word.

(b) 'do not fear' v. 1: struggled with this – trying to name the things I do fear. Perhaps shame – the revelation of my own failures?

(c) 'You are mine' v. 1. Just felt this as a promise.

(d) 'burned' v. 3: not sure what this was about either – bad times? Receiving the gift of the Spirit? A process of purging and cleansing? The promise seems to be of hope through such things.

(e) 'honoured' v. 4: what does it mean to be 'honoured' in God's sight? Another promise against shame?

(f) 'daughters' v. 6: spent time praying for [my own daughters], and for my own role as their father.

Each word or phrase was a place where I felt I needed to stop and respond as I prayed. These notes represent about 25 minutes of praying with the passage, according to my notebook; looking through that book, as the retreat continued, some of the themes, particularly the question 'what do I fear?' became recurrent, and I reflected more deeply and understood better as time went on.

Another way of praying with Scripture, popularized by St Ignatius of Loyola, uses the visual imagination to become part of a Biblical narrative or scene. Typically, the pray-er imagines herself to be a part of the crowd or group, whoever they may be (perhaps Jesus' disciples) in the passage, and watches the events unfold – seeing, hearing, smelling, tasting, touching, feeling what is going on. St Ignatius used this method to read gospel narratives, and suggested that the imaginative pray-er ends with an imagined encounter with Christ, which builds on what has gone before.

This works less well for me – I don't have a particularly vivid visual imagination. Indeed, looking at my notebook for the day after the prayer time I described above, I tried to pray like this, and recorded 'Found imagination difficult – the prayer was more like writing a novel about being there than being there'. My notes on the prayer, however, went like this (I was imagining myself as one of John's disciples who went after Jesus):

John – wild-eyed and unpredictable – busy-ness – singling out one from among all the people – hesitantly following him. 'What do you want?' – my answer: to be with him. Then the rest of the day – an impression of being with Jesus in the ordinary things of life (he was preparing a meal; I was just sitting there) – that sense of wanting the presence of Jesus was the major impression. Then the ending. Wanting to know where he was going, to be with him – a sense that I couldn't know in advance, but if I really wanted to be with him, I'd always be able to find him – this a big part of the response – struggling with what this might mean.

These are classic ways of praying with Scripture imaginatively, but it's not hard to think up others. Can you sing the passage, or choose and sing worship songs that express what you find in the passage? (If there aren't any suitable songs, why not? What are our songbooks missing?) Can you paint the passage? Could you write a response, or re-tell the story in your own words, in a way that brings out the meaning for you (see Bob Hartman's wonderful *Telling the Bible* (Monarch, 2006) for some great examples of what this could look like)? None of these are right or wrong: hearing sermons and painting pictures are both just ways of trying to open up your heart and life so that God's word in Scripture can impact on you in a creative and life-changing way. Again, the point is – whatever works for you. With the Bible too, we each need to find the right running shoes.

The rest of this book

Most of this book is made up of forty extracts from a few spiritual writers from across the history of the church. Men and women, lay and ordained, shut away from the world or right in the middle of the world's greatest cities – they are very different people. We have deliberately restricted ourselves to a few writers, so that if you read all the extracts you will meet each writer several times and get to know them a little. (We have included brief biographies of each of them at the end of the book.) If you have read some of them before, you might find our texts surprising – we have re-translated or paraphrased them into more immediate, modern English than is normally used in publications (our model was Eugene Peterson's *The Message* translation of the Bible).

The extracts are divided up into four sets of ten, each exploring a different theme: 'Learning', 'Living', 'Working' and 'Growing'. Under the heading 'Learning', we have included extracts that talk about the different ways in which God meets us and instructs us, leads us on. As different people, we learn in different ways. These readings give you insight into how some of God's children through history have understood God's call to learn from him, how they have felt him teaching them.

The readings in the section on 'Living' explore how the things we say we believe should affect the way we live our lives, and how the lifestyle choices we make reveal our true beliefs. The deepest commitments of our hearts are demonstrated by a thousand seemingly trivial choices we make – each one in itself almost irrelevant, but building together into a revealing account of what actually matters to us. Equally, deliberate lifestyle choices can re-educate our desires and assumptions, and can eventually change our heart-beliefs.

Under 'Growing' we are offered the invitation to grow closer to God, and more effective in our discipleship in the world. The closer we come to God's beating heart of love, which is the fundamental reality of the universe, the more we will be committed to living out that love in the world, and in every situation in which we find ourselves. Those who are detached from God are detached from the world; those who begin by turning their backs on worldly things to seize hold of God find in the end that God's grace compels them to a full involvement with the world, in service and evangelism.

Finally, under 'Working,' we give readings that explore the dynamic relationship between the freedom that God has given us in Jesus and the call to follow and obey, to find rules and disciplines of life that lead us further into that freedom and life. God's gifts and our efforts are not opposed, but work together to lead us further into God's purposes.

You will realize if you read these extracts carefully that these people do not always agree. At certain points, they give straight-forwardly contradictory advice. This is a reflection of their different contexts and temperaments. Perhaps you will discover here a kindred spirit – that Mother Julian, John Bunyan or Catherine Booth describes the way of following Jesus in language that speaks directly to your heart. If so, the Bibliography at the end will point you to further resources. Perhaps you will understand the different concerns of each writer, recognizing the worth of Bunyan and à Kempis's severity, the engagement of Catherine Booth, and the focus on love offered by Brother Lawrence or Julian of Norwich. It does not particularly matter: being the person you are, some things will help you and some things will not. Your task – God's call on you – is to discover and to act on what works for you. Your task is to pray as you can, not as you can't.

We offer you the readings as texts that might help you in prayer for a few days. After everything that has come before, it will be no surprise to learn that we are not going to tell you how to use these extracts. You might read one before or as part of each of your regular prayer times. You might pray through them, using the *lectio divina* technique above. You might choose to read one a day at a time other than your normal prayer time. You might read the whole set quickly, then pick one or two that interest, puzzle, or excite you, and read those several times each through the week. They are a resource – a resource giving wisdom from people who all walked closely with God and had lives visibly shaped by God's love. They lived in different places and times, had different calls upon them, and different personalities and temperaments; as a result, they prayed and met God in different ways. Our hope and prayer is that they will inspire you to find a spirituality that works for you, a way of placing yourself – day by day and week by week – in the presence of God, so that the Holy Spirit can re-create and integrate your life.

STEPHEN R. HOLMES
St Andrews
September 2008

SECTION ONE

✛

LEARNING

Chapter One

All or Nothing

THIS EXTRACT HAS BEEN TAKEN FROM THE
'CONVERSATIONS OF BROTHER LAWRENCE'.

Brother Lawrence told me that we should fix ourselves in God's presence by constantly talking with him; it is disgraceful to joke and gossip instead of talking with God.

We should feed our spirits with big pictures of God – this will bring us much joy in living for him.

We should bring our faith to life! What a shame we have so little faith! Instead of taking faith as the one principle to govern our lives, we play around with petty devotions, changing them every day. The beating heart of Christ's Church is the way of faith, and this alone is enough to lead us to perfect maturity.

We ought to abandon ourselves to God – completely, fully! We ought to give ourselves to God in our work and home and leisure as much as in our prayers and worship. We should never be satisfied with anything other than doing what God wants, whether he takes us down a difficult path or an easy one. It makes no difference to someone who is wholly committed to God. God proves our love for him by making the way hard for a time; we need to be faithful in these times. It's precisely in these hard times that we can choose to trust God and not ourselves – doing this just once would do us so much good!

Brother Lawrence said he heard of troubles and sins every day. They didn't surprise him; instead he was amazed that worse didn't happen, considering how bad sinners could be. He prayed for whatever situations he heard of, but he knew that God could change them if he wanted to, so he did not worry any more about them.

If we want to give ourselves up to God the way God calls us to, we must be aware of every emotion and thought – always there are good things mixed with bad in them. God will help us to make sense of what we feel if we really want to serve him. Brother Lawrence ended by saying he would always be there for me if I really wanted to serve God – but if I didn't, I should not bother him again.

More to think and pray ...

1. Do our conversations with God require a different type of language? While few would suggest that disciples need to use super-spiritual language in their prayer lives it must surely be possible and preferable for us to develop a deeply personal and intimate approach to prayer?

2. As with Brother Lawrence, can you identify a time when your faith has been strengthened by a period of personal hardship? With the benefit of this hindsight reflect on present challenges and how God might be using these to enhance your walk with him.

3. Without wishing to 'bother' anyone, are there friends that we should be asking for help and assistance as we try to follow Jesus in the here and now?

The Book of Common Prayer

'Blessed Lord, who has called all holy Scriptures to be written for our learning; Grant that we may in such wise hear them, read, mark, learn, and inwardly digest them, that by patience, and comfort of thy holy Word, we may embrace, and ever hold fast the blessed hope of everlasting life.'

Collects, The Second Sunday in Advent

Chapter Two

Cut to the Heart

THIS EXTRACT IS TAKEN FROM A SERMON ON ROMANS 2:29 BY JOHN WESLEY, ENTITLED 'THE CIRCUMCISION OF THE HEART'. IT WAS FIRST PREACHED AT OXFORD UNIVERSITY ON NEW YEAR'S DAY, 1773.

... A true Jew is one whose heart is right with God. And true circumcision is not merely obeying the letter of the law; rather, it is a change of heart produced by God's Spirit. And a person with a changed heart seeks praise from God, not from people. [Rom. 2:29, NLT]

The 'circumcision' that Paul calls for demands the total transformation of our hearts by God's Spirit as opposed to a simple physical compliance with the letter of the Law. For the distinguishing features of God's people are not the physical signs of circumcision, baptism, or any other outward mark but a mind, soul and spirit renewed by and for the Creator....

As Paul suggests, rather than chasing the cheers of men we should rest content and wait for the day of God's coming. On this day we will hear his loud, 'Well done!' and receive his own rapturous applause in the sight of men and angels.

The circumcision of the heart calls for humility, faith, hope and love. The secret of humility is true self-awareness, freedom from conceit and resistance to the delusions of grandeur that accompany our achievements, whether they are few or many. Such confessions prevent us from believing that we are rich, wise, or in any other way self-sufficient. They convince us that, at best, we are filled with sin and vanity; that confusion, and ignorance, and error continue to reign over our understanding; that irrational, selfish and sensual passions undermine our best intentions and usurp our will. In addition, they remind us that we cannot rescue ourselves. Without God's transforming Spirit, we can do nothing but pile new sin on old. Without God's work and his almighty power our lives come to no good. If even one good thought proves beyond us, how can we begin our journey to redemption, renewal and righteousness? The answer is clear, by the supernatural assistance of God's Spirit....

We who are born again by faith in Christ have the great consolation of his hope. This is the next thing we learn from Paul's circumcision of the heart. Because of the Spirit's work in us we have become the Children of God. By his Holy Spirit, God has redirected our hearts towards him and our actions to please him. By his mercy we have been rerouted along the path of life and with his strength we will reach the end. We can walk this road eagerly in the lively expectation that all good things come from God's hand, anticipating as we go the joyful prospect of an eternal reward, the crown of glory reserved for us in heaven. By holding firm to this hope, we can remain steady amid the storms of life ...

True disciples are not discouraged by a hard race or by a difficult fight. Neither do we expect the going to be easy nor demand less than all our strength. However, we know that our effort is not in vain, that we are joined in this race and aided in this fight by God's people. Paul, the great Apostle of the Gentiles, offers his own example by way of a 'team talk' ...

> Run to win! All athletes are disciplined in their training. [Some] do it to win a prize that will fade away, but we do it for an eternal prize. So I run with purpose in every step. I am not just shadowboxing. I discipline my body like an athlete, training it to do what it should. Otherwise, I fear that after preaching to others I myself might be disqualified. [1 Cor. 9:24–27, NLT]

By the same discipline every good disciple must learn to endure hardship. Only then, when every appetite and aspiration has been mastered, will we be able to defeat the darkness. By God's grace, our daily routines must be designed to purge and purify every detail of or our lives. There can be no place for lust, selfishness, jealousy, envy, bitterness, malice nor any other baggage that would slow our run or hamper our fight. Our very bodies are the temple of God, the place in which his Spirit dwells, hence nothing should be allowed to taint or defile them ...

To all this, the disciple must add love. Add love, and you have the circumcision of the heart. Love is the fulfilment of the whole law and the end of every commandment (Rom. 13:10). Most excellent things are said of love; it is the essence, the spirit, the life of all virtue. It is not only the first and great command, but it is all the commandments in one. If we wish to win this race we must fix our eyes on 'love'. For all that 'is true, and honourable, and right, and pure, and lovely and admirable' is comprised in that one word (Phil. 4:8). In this we find perfection, glory and happiness. Hence the royal law of heaven states, 'Love the Lord your God with all your heart, all your soul, and all your strength' (Deut. 6:4).

This doesn't prohibit the disciple from loving anything else. In fact, it insists that we love our brothers and sisters also. Neither does it deprive us from taking pleasure in other things.... What it does mean is that there is one perfect love that comprises our ultimate end. There is one thing that we should desire above all else, one happiness that we propose for our souls and one design that we pursue to the end of time; to enjoy loving fellowship with the Father, Son and Holy Spirit in time and eternity. True disciples may desire other things, so long as they move us towards love, the glorious finishing line of living faith. We should love creation and creatures, in such a way that it leads us to the Creator and hence, submit all thoughts and affections, words and works to him. Whatever we desire or fear, whatever we seek, or shun, whatever we think, speak, or do may it bring happiness to our God, the sole End and Source of our being.

More to think and pray ...

1. Self-awareness is one of the secrets of successful discipleship. How self-aware are you? Do you have a realistic sense of your value and worth, strengths and weaknesses? Why not ask God, and those around you if you are brave enough, to provide some kind of appraisal of your discipleship?

2. Which appetites have you yet to master along life's way? Rather than being continually dictated by destructive temptations and bad habits, consider strategies to break free and think about those around you who might provide helpful accountability.

3. Lastly, how might you add more love to your life? Think about those who you struggle to love and commit to, going out of your way to express care and concern for them as an act of love and worship to God.

Reading

Reading is a key part of the life of the monk in Benedict's *Rule*; St Teresa stresses the value of books to her nuns. Books have always been important aids to Christian discipleship. The Bible is at the heart of this, of course, but other books are also helpful. If we find a writer who expresses her insights in a way that suits our ways of thinking, or who describes creating a life of discipleship in circumstances not too different to our own, they can act like a good preacher, helping us to relate the truths of Scripture to our own lives, when Scripture sometimes seems so foreign from us.

Of course, the writers in this volume did not have the technology we have. I am sure they would have included podcasts and audiobooks if they had known about them. I think they would have counselled us against 'multitasking': Benedict would not have wanted the brothers to listen to Scripture or a preacher while working, because work has its own value, and we should not be distracted from it. We need to focus on the words, concentrate, and think about them. It is more important to read (or listen) deeply than widely – and much more important still to put what we learn into practice!

Chapter Three

How God Leads

THIS EXTRACT COMES FROM THE AUTOBIOGRAPHY
OF TERESA OF AVILA.

I was tired of religion, and I had developed bad habits which made me restless, even though I wanted peace. One day, I went into the chapel and saw a picture that had been left there, ready for a holy day that the house was going to mark. It showed Christ brutally wounded but submissive and worshipful. It showed how He had suffered for us so well that I was moved by the sight of it. I felt how badly I had neglected what He had done, so much so that I was almost broken. I threw myself on the ground, crying openly, and begged Christ to strengthen me once for all, so that I should never do anything to grieve Him any more.

I used to think very often of Mary Magdalene, and particularly of her conversion. I always thought about this when I received communion – I knew for certain then that the Lord was with me, and so I would place myself at His feet, trusting that my tears would not be despised as hers were not. I never really knew what I was saying – only that He did great things for me. He was pleased, I believe, that I should shed those tears, but I soon forgot this feeling.

But this time, in front of the picture I described, I think I made some progress. After this I stopped trusting myself, and put all my confidence in God. I think that I said to Him that I would not get up until he had given me what I asked. This was a significant moment for me: I have grown better ever since.

This is how I prayed: I could not think very well, so I tried to imagine Christ within me. I used to find thinking about those times in His life when He was most lonely helped me to grow.

I felt more able to approach Him when I thought of Him alone and troubled. I did lots of simple things like this in prayer. In particular, I used to like to pray in the Garden of Gethsemane with Him. I thought of His bloody sweat, of the pain he suffered there; I wanted to wipe the sweat away from His face, but I remember that I never dared to do this – my sins were too obvious to me. I would stay there with Him as long as my thoughts allowed me – many thoughts troubled me, though. For many years I used to think a little of this prayer in the Garden nearly every night when I prayed before sleep. I did this even before I was a nun, because I was told it would do me good. I think I gained much from it, because I began to pray even before I knew what prayer was, and it became a habit with me.

This method of praying, which does not involve much thought, might be very helpful, or very dangerous to us. If instead of thinking we are filled with love, we will make great progress in prayer. But it costs us to get there (as I say, I was troubled by many thoughts when I began). There are a few people, indeed, who God is pleased to lead to contemplation quickly – I know some. For those who walk this way, a book is often helpful to bring us home to ourselves. I found looking on fields, water or flowers helped me – I saw traces of the Creator in them. Such sights were like a book for me, they roused me, brought me back to myself, and reminded me of my ingratitude and my sins. My mind was so dull that I could never imagine heavenly or worthwhile things in any way until God showed them to me in another way.

Unless I saw a thing with my eyes, I could not imagine it. So I couldn't do as others do and bring myself back together by imagining the things of God. I could only think of Christ as a man – I could not form any image of Him in my mind, although I read lots about His beauty and even looked at pictures of Him. It was as if I was blind, or in the dark – I was speaking to someone who I knew was present, I could sense His presence; I mean, I knew Him to be present, and believed it –but I could not see Him. That's how it was for me when I used to think of our Lord, and that is why I enjoyed images so much …

About this time, someone gave me St Augustine's *Confessions*. This must have been God's doing, because I wasn't looking for the book, and indeed had never seen it before. I was devoted to

St Augustine, because I lived in a monastery that was part of the Order he had founded, and also because he had been a notorious sinner. I used to find much comfort in saints who the Lord turned to Himself after they had sinned. I thought that the Lord might forgive me, as He had forgiven them. I worried, though, that our Lord had called them only once, and they had never fallen back. I had fallen so often! This troubled me, but I would remember the Lord's love for me and take courage. I never once doubted His mercy – I doubted myself.

O my God, I am amazed how hard my heart was, in the face of so much help from you! I am terrified when I see how weak I was, how blocked, so that I could not decide to give myself completely to you! When I began to read the *Confessions*, I felt he was telling the story of my life. When I came to the story of his conversion, and read how he had heard a voice in the garden, it seemed to me that God had spoken it for me, it affected me so deeply. I was lost for a while in tears, troubled and distressed.

O my God, we have to suffer so much because we no longer are in control of ourselves! What pain we have to endure! I marvel now how I managed to live in such pain; but God be praised, who gave me life, so that I escaped this evil death! I believe that God's divine majesty gave me great strength at that time, that He heard my cry and had compassion on my tears.

More to think and pray ...

1. Teresa talks about the difficulties she had with the ways she had been taught to pray; what advice have you received that actually hinders you from praying?
2. Is there a book or a talk you have heard that God used to tell you the truth about your own condition, and to lead you on?
3. Which scenes from the Gospels help you to pray particularly?

Chapter Four

Abounding Grace

THIS EXTRACT IS TAKEN FROM 'GRACE ABOUNDING TO THE CHIEF OF SINNERS', THE TESTIMONY OF JOHN BUNYAN, AUTHOR OF *THE PILGRIM'S PROGRESS*.

As I walked along, my conscience became troubled and, fearing that something wasn't right, I stumbled upon this sentence, 'Your righteousness is in heaven.' With this, my soul caught sight of Jesus Christ, sitting at the right hand of the Father and suddenly I realized where my own righteousness lay. Wherever I go and whatever I do from here, God knows I am righteous because my righteousness is guaranteed by his Son. What's more, my best behaviour does not add to my righteousness and neither does my worst diminish it. For my righteousness is Jesus Christ and as such remains the same, yesterday, today, forever (Heb. 13:8).

In this moment, my chains fell off, I was freed from the afflictions of false guilt and my many temptations ran away. The most terrifying judgements and damnations left me and I went home rejoicing in God's love and grace. Arriving home I tried to find the verse, 'Your righteousness is in heaven.' Unable to locate it my heart sank but then I remembered what Paul had written in 1 Corinthians 1:30. Jesus has become our 'wisdom, righteousness, holiness and redemption' [NIV]. Praise God! It's true!

I realized that in reaching out for Christ – the human who is both like us in our humanity and yet different from us through his perfection – we can take hold of the true righteousness and holiness which is his before God. Here, at peace with God in Christ, I lived most sweetly for some time. Jesus! Jesus! I could see nothing but Jesus, his holiness and wholeness; his life, death and resurrection; all of his features and friendships, miracles and ministries enthroned in heaven at the right hand of God (Eph. 1:3).

Christ's exaltation was a glorious sight to me. What's more, I could now see that those small works which God had begun in me were like pocket change to a millionaire. While I may have little on me at present, Christ has deposited huge sums of gold into my heavenly savings account. From this moment on Jesus literally meant everything to me: all my wisdom, all my righteousness, all my sanctification, and all my redemption.

In all this, I learned the secret of union with God: I am one with God through Christ. As part of his body, I share his flesh and bones (Eph. 5:30). And if he and I are one, then his righteousness, merits and victory also belong to me. I can now see myself in heaven and on earth – in heaven with Christ as my head and on earth in body and person.

I could also now see Christ as God sees him: as the one through whom God views all of his people. In Jesus we have kept and fulfilled God's law. In him we have risen from the dead, defeated sin and become victorious over death and the devil. When Jesus died, we died. When he rose, we rose (Is. 26:19; Hos. 6:2). When Christ took his seat in heaven, we were seated with him (Eph. 2:6).

These beautiful pictures and bright shining revelations left me speechless save only to exclaim ...

Praise the LORD! Praise God in His sanctuary; Praise Him in His mighty firmament! Praise Him for His mighty acts; Praise Him according to His excellent greatness. (Ps. 150:1–2)

More to think and pray ...

1. Have you ever experienced a powerful moment of revelation? Reflect on the lessons that this experience has taught you.
2. Take a moment to reflect on the phrase, 'My righteousness is in heaven,' or meditate on 1 Corinthians 1:30. Be encouraged that your eternal standing before God rests not on your own achievements but what Jesus himself achieved as God's beloved Son in his death and resurrection.

3. Take time to read Psalm 150 and/or use it as a template to improvise your own Psalm of Praise.

Some (possibly …) interesting prayer ideas

1. Write a psalm.
2. Draw or paint your prayer.
3. Find a way of expressing your prayer physically using arms, legs, posture, movement.
4. Go for a prayer walk – begin by 'centring down,' and asking God to guide your mind as you walk. Then walk and pray – around a park or through a town or wherever.
5. Cut a few interesting or arresting pictures out of a newspaper or magazine, then let them lead you in prayer.
6. Spend your time reading a whole book of Scripture quickly. You might read a short book every day for a week, or a longer book a couple of times a week for a month. Feel the flow, the shape, the big picture of the book (I remember the first time I read Acts through at one sitting, realizing just how *exciting* the story is).
7. Give a whole week to praying again and again and again through the same few verses of Scripture.
8. Pray somewhere you don't normally. At work, or on a train, or just in the kitchen. Does it make a difference? Why?
9. Pray in a different posture. If you normally sit to pray, try standing, or kneeling (if you are up to it physically …). Again, what difference, if any, does it make?
10. If you normally pray silently, pray out loud today. If you normally pray out loud, pray silently.
11. Write God a letter. Or send him some text messages.
12. Take an alarm clock – or use your watch, or mobile phone – with you today, set to go off every hour. Every time it rings (beeps, vibrates …) stop what you are doing and pray, even if only for a moment or two.
13. Pray through your desk, or kitchen table. Pick up each item or piece of paper; how might it lead you in prayer? Does it remind you of someone who needs God's help, of a situation that needs prayer, of something to be thankful for, of your own failures – what? Respond in prayer.

Chapter Five

Agony and Love

THESE POEMS ARE TAKEN FROM *THE TEMPLE*,
BY GEORGE HERBERT.

The Agonie
Philosophers have measured mountains,
Fathomed the depths of seas, of states, and kings,
Walked with a staff to heaven, and traced fountains:
    But there are two vast, spacious things,
The which to measure it doth more behove:[1]
Yet few there are that sound them; Sin and Love.

    Who would know Sin, let him repair
Unto mount Olivet; there shall he see
A man so wrung with pains, that all his hair,
    His skin, his garments bloody be.
Sin is that press and vice, which forces pain
To hunt his cruel food through every vein.

    Who knows not Love, let him assay
And taste that juice, which on the cross a pike
Did set again abroach;[2] then let him say
    If ever he did taste the like.
Love in that liquour sweet and most divine,
Which my God feels as blood; but I, as wine.

---

[1] 'It doth more behove' means 'it is better to'.
[2] 'Abroach': as in 'broaching a cask of beer': opening to let the liquid out.

Love

Love bade me welcome: yet my soul drew back,
            Guilty of dust and sin.
But quick-eyed Love, observing me grow slack
            From my first entrance in,
Drew nearer to me, sweetly questioning,
            If I lacked any thing.

A guest, I answered, worthy to be here:
            Love said, You shall be he.
I the unkind, ungrateful? Ah my dear,
            I cannot look on thee.
Love took my hand, and smiling did reply,
            Who made the eyes but I?

Truth Lord, but I have marred them: let my shame
            Go where it doth deserve.
And know you not, says Love, who bore the blame?
            My dear, then I will serve.
You must sit down, says Love, and taste my meat:
            So I did sit and eat.

The Elixir

Teach me, my God and King,
    In all things thee to see,
And what I do in any thing,
    To do it as for thee:

Not rudely, as a beast,
    To run into an action;
But still to make thee prepossessed,
    And give it his perfection.

A man that looks on glass,
    On it may stay his eye;
Or if he pleaseth, through it pass,
    And then the heaven espy.

All may of thee partake:
Nothing can be so mean,
Which with his tincture (for thy sake)
Will not grow bright and clean.

A servant with this clause
Makes drudgery divine:
Who sweeps a room, as for thy laws,
Makes that and the action fine.

This is the famous stone
That turneth all to gold:
For that which God doth touch and own
Cannot for less be told.

More to think and pray ...

1. Herbert suggests we understand the nature of sin not from our own lives, but from looking at Christ's cross; how does that make you feel?
2. Can you think of times in your own life when you have sensed God more ready to welcome than you were to come?
3. Would consciously doing your chores and work as an offering to God make a difference to you?

Chapter Six

Gaining Christ

THESE EXTRACTS WERE TAKEN FROM *THE IMITATION OF CHRIST* BY THOMAS À KEMPIS.

Imitating Christ, and disdaining all the world's fripperies

1. 'Whoever follows me does not walk in the dark,' says the Lord [Jn. 8:12]. These are Christ's words – advice to copy his way of life, if we want to walk in his light, free of inner blindness. And so our minds should be full of one thing: the life of Jesus Christ.

2. Christ's teaching is so much better than the teaching of any other holy teacher! If you have His Spirit you will find hidden manna there. But so many feel almost no desire for it even though they hear the Gospels so often – it's because they lack Christ's Spirit! But anyone who wants a deep and satisfying grasp of Christ's words needs to strive to match their whole life to Christ.

3. What use is it to argue cleverly about the Trinity, if you lack humility, and so grieve the Trinity? Get this: clever words don't make a saint, or even a Christian! No, God is pleased with people who live well. I'd rather feel my sin and shame, not understand it! You might know every word of the Bible, and have degrees and doctorates, but all that gains you precisely nothing without the love and grace of God. 'Everything is pretty bling and fake show' except loving God, and serving Him and Him alone [Eccl. 1:2]. This is real wisdom, reaching out for the Kingdom of God by despising the world.

4. So it is pointless to get rich and to hope that will help you. Status and honours and titles are worthless too! Sex and drugs seem like fun for a while, but just lead to suffering. Don't hope for a long life – strive for a good life! And don't get stuck on this life – think about the life to come! It's pointless to love things that will vanish quickly, instead of aiming for the place where eternal joys will last.

5. Keep remembering the proverb: 'seeing is not enough for the eye, and the ear wants more than sound' [Eccl. 1:8]. You need to work to stop loving worldly things that you can see, and to start loving heavenly things, which you can't see. This is important, because everyone who just follows brutish desires loses both the ability to know what is right, and God's grace!

Why so few love the cross of Christ

1. These days, Jesus has many who love his heavenly kingdom – but few who carry His cross. He has many who want to feel good – but few who want to struggle. He finds more to feast with Him; few to fast with Him. All want to share His joy; few want to bear His troubles. Many follow Jesus to the breaking of bread – but few to drinking the cup of suffering. Many goggle at His miracles; few follow the shame of the cross. Many love Jesus when it is easy. Many praise and bless Him, so long as they get something from Him. But if Jesus hides Himself, just for a moment, they grumble and are discouraged.

2. But those who love Jesus, and not just what they get from Jesus, worship Him in trouble and suffering, just as they do when most aware of His blessing. If He chose never to let them know His blessing, they would still always praise Him, and always want to be grateful.

3. The pure love of Jesus is so powerful, if it is not watered down with any selfish love! Aren't those who are always looking for blessings just mercenary? Doesn't this just show that they love themselves more than Christ? They only ever think of their own advantage, their own gains! Isn't there anyone who is willing to serve God for nothing?

4. There are very few people so spiritual that they are stripped of everything. Is anyone truly poor in spirit, and detached from everything created? If someone has given away everything, it is still nothing; doing great penance is only a small thing; someone who knows everything is still far away; the most virtuous person, whose devotion burns like fire, still lacks so much. There is one thing, one thing that matters more than all the rest. What is it? Having given up everything, we give up ourselves. We need to leave ourselves behind, lose every trace of self-love. And when we have done everything we can think of, we should still feel that we have not begun.

5. We should not pay much attention to what things look like, but instead acknowledge the truth that we are unworthy servants. The Truth says 'When you have done everything that has been set for you, say, we are unworthy servants.' Then you will really be poor in spirit, and stripped bare, and with the Prophet you can say 'I am poor and needy.' But no-one is richer, no-one more powerful, no-one more free, than someone who knows how to surrender himself and everything else, and see himself as the lowest of all.

More to think and pray ...

1. How do we respond to the challenge to fill our lives with Christ? Presuming that this doesn't happen by accident, take some time to consider one significant part of your life. How might Christ be more central to your family life, leisure time, daily routine, monthly budget, etc?

2. How important is it for you to win an argument, be seen to have more knowledge or be revered for your wisdom? How might you develop greater humility as you progress your walk with Christ?

3. All too often, life in the Western world appears to be one long competition to see who can accumulate the most toys before we die. When was the last time that you intentionally practiced simplicity and sought to find freedom in owning less and giving away more? By walking in the opposite direction to so much

of our culture we increase our chances of meeting Jesus, the one who gave up his throne in heaven for a cross on Calvary.

Getting Ready to Pray: Centring Techniques

One thing that the classic texts on prayer almost always teach is a set of ways to prepare for prayer. Like everything else, these might not help you, but they do seem to help many people. They are different ways of quietening down enough to be in a place to sense the presence of God. Most of us, most of the time, have thoughts chasing each other through our minds so rapidly that there is no space to hear God's still, small, insistent whisper. Centring techniques are ways to be ready to pray. There are lots of them. Here are some:

1. *Breathing*: as you sit quietly preparing to pray, become aware of your breathing. Don't try to force it or control; just feel the rhythm that is always there, but usually unconscious. Focus on it for a while, as a way of leaving other thoughts behind and becoming still and quiet. You might find using a simple prayer with each breath helps: letting go of the troubles and worries of the day as you breathe out, and asking God to fill you with His love and His Spirit as you breathe in, perhaps. After a minute or two, you should find yourself more prepared to pray than you were before.

2. *Repeating a simple prayer*: You might try repeating a simple prayer, or a quiet, one- or two-line song, over and over, as a way of slowing and stopping the constant stream of thoughts that run through your mind. Some of the music from the Taizé community works well for this, or a one-line prayer like 'Lord Jesus, Son of God, have mercy on me'.

3. *Listen to the noises around*: When you sit down to pray, spend a few moments just becoming aware of the noises around you. Hear each one, name it, and dismiss it. When you are comfortable with the silence (or lack of it) begin to pray.

4. *Relax your muscles*: Starting with your feet, tense up the muscles and then consciously relax them, letting go of tension. Move up your legs, doing the same thing, through your torso, emphasize your shoulders, where so much tension collects, and work down your arms and into the muscles of your neck and face. When you are finished, begin to pray.

Chapter Seven

God's Knowledge and Ours

THIS EXTRACT IS TAKEN FROM *REVELATIONS OF DIVINE LOVE*, BY MOTHER JULIAN OF NORWICH.

In this passing life we know only what we can see, so we do not know what we really are. In the next life we will see rightly and clearly, we will know our Lord God, and be full of joy. It is inevitable, then, that the closer we are to true happiness, the greater our longing will be. We can know something of ourselves here through the constant help and strength of the best parts of our souls. We can grow this knowledge, increase it – and God's mercy and grace make this growth possible, and call us to it – but we can never know ourselves completely until the very last moment, when this passing life, full of pain and sorrow, will be over. Because of this, it is right for us to desire, to long with all our strength, to know ourselves in the fullness of eternal joy.

Yet in all this time, from the beginning to the end of the vision, I saw in two very different ways. On the one hand, I had a sense of endless love, and complete certainty of God's care, and His holy salvation. This was luminously clear in every moment of the vision. On the other, I remembered the normal teaching of the holy church, which I had previously learnt. I willingly applied this, and understood it further through the vision. And I never stopped thinking about this, because the vision did not differ from the church's teaching at all. So I learnt through the vision to love the church's doctrine, to appreciate it more. Through concentrating on it, I believe the Lord will help me to rise to greater love, and holier knowledge.

From all this, I grasped that we have to see ourselves rightly, to know that we are sinners. We do all sorts of evil that we ought to have left, and we leave many good deeds that we ought to have done. And we deserve to suffer for this, to feel God's anger.

But despite all this, I saw that the Lord is never angry, and never will be. He is God: goodness; life; truth; love; peace! His love will not allow Him to be angry, and He cannot be angry if He remains true to Himself. Let me explain this: I saw that He cannot be angry and mighty at the same time, and He cannot be angry and wise, or angry and good at the same time. Now God is the goodness that cannot be angry – that is just who He is. We are united to His goodness, and so in God's eyes there can be nothing, nothing at all between Him and us.

In every vision I was led by love, drawn by strength to this same knowledge: this is what our good Lord showed to me, and this is what is – all because of His great goodness. He wants us to long to know this truth, to long to see this truth, as far as we can know it. God wants to reveal, wants us to know, everything that our hearts can understand of Him. As for the rest, He wants to keep them secret. He does this, so we know it is wise, and done only from love for us. I saw in this same vision that there are many mysteries hidden; they will be kept hidden until God in His goodness makes us worthy to see them. I am happy with this, completely happy: it is God's will, and I cheerfully submit to it. And I submit to the teachings of the church also, just as a simple child does.

More to think and pray ...

1. 'The closer we are to true happiness, the greater our longing will be.' How can this make sense?
2. Julian stresses that there was nothing in her visions that contradicted the teachings of the church; How important does this seem to you?
3. 'The Lord is never angry.' Think and pray about this.

Chapter Eight

Honour and Shame

THIS EXTRACT WAS TAKEN FROM THE WRITINGS OF THE DESERT FATHERS.

The holy bishop Basil [of Caesarea] told this story: there was a community of nuns where there was a girl who pretended to be mad, and even to be possessed. She was so scorned by the other sisters that they would not even eat with her, which she was very happy about. She lived in the kitchen and took all the worst jobs. She was what they used to call 'the sponge of the house'.

By living like this, she was fulfilling the Scripture which says 'If anyone among you seems to be wise in this world, they should become a fool so that they can be wise'. She always wore a rag tied around her head, whereas all the others had their hair cut short and wore hoods. She would serve them dressed like that. Not one of the four hundred women there ever saw her eat in all the years of her life. She never sat at table or ate any bread; she wiped the crumbs from the tables and scraped out the cooking pots. She never did any harm to anyone; no-one ever heard her complain. She never gossiped or chattered at all. She was beaten by all, she lived with the hatred of all, and bore the curses of all.

The Lord saw all this and sent an angel to the holy Pyoterius, the famous hermit who lived near Porphyrite. The angel said to him, 'Why do you think so much of yourself, living in a place like this. Do you want to see a woman who is holier than you are? Go to Tabennisi, to the female monastery there, and you will find someone with a cloth wrapped around her head. Know that she is better than you are! She is beaten by many, day and night, but she has never let her heart turn from God. But you live here alone, yet your heart and your thoughts are back in the cities'.

So he went to the monastery and asked to be let into the women's house. He was old, and had a great reputation, so they let him in confidently. He went in and asked to see all the sisters, but the woman he wanted to see did not appear. Finally he said to them 'Bring them all to me! I want to see the one who is missing!' They said to him, 'Well, we have an imbecile in the kitchen ...' (This is what they used to call someone afflicted by demons.) He said 'Bring her to me also; I want to see her.' So they went to call her, but she would not answer. Somehow she knew what was going on – I believe it might be because God revealed it to her. They grabbed her and told her 'The holy Pyoterius wants to see you' (he was famous, after all).

When she came in he saw the rag on her head and fell at her feet, saying 'Bless me!' Then she fell at his feet, saying, 'Bless me, my lord!' All the sisters were amazed, and said, 'Do not let her insult you, Father – she is touched.' Pyoterius then said to them all, 'You are foolish, not her! This woman is a Mother to me and to you! I only pray that I may be found as worthy as she is on the day of judgement!' When they heard this, they threw themselves at his feet, confessing different things. One said that she had poured the leftovers on her plate over her; another that she had struck her; another that she had burned her nose. So they confessed their various cruelties. The holy man prayed for them all, and then left.

A few days later, she was unable to cope with the praises and honour the sisters gave her, or to put up with all their apologizing. So she left the monastery. Where she went and how she died, nobody knows....

✠

A brother at Scetis was getting ready to bring in the harvest, and he went to a great Father and said to him, 'Father, tell me what I should do – should I go to harvest?' The Father said to him, 'If I tell you, will you trust me?' The brother said, 'I will listen to you.'

The Father said to him, 'If you trust me, give up this harvesting, come here, and I will tell you what to do.' So the brother gave up harvesting and came to live with the Father. The Father said to him, 'Go into your cell and spend fifty days eating only dry bread and salt once a day. Then I will tell you something else to do.' The brother went away, did this, then came back to the Father. The Father, seeing that he was truly committed, taught him how to live in the cell.

So the brother went away to his cell. There he fell face down on the ground and wept before God for three days and three nights. After this, the thought came to him, 'You are finished, you have become a great man!' but he remembered his sins and said 'And where are all the things I have forgotten?' But when the opposite thought came to him, 'You have committed so many sins!' he simply said, 'But I say my prayers, and I believe that he will be merciful.'

In this way, he conquered the evil spirits, who came to him openly and said 'You have confused us!' He asked them why, and they said, 'When we lift you up, you run into humility, but when we try to humiliate you, you rise up.'

More to think and pray ...

1. How guilty are we of making judgements based on appearances and preconceived ideas? How can we live differently?

2. In your community, what types of people, behaviour or achievements are usually praised and rewarded? How might you identify and affirm those whose growth, efforts and industry go largely unseen and unremarked upon?

3. While some Christians struggle to acquire humility, others find it hard to overcome humiliation. Which of these presents the greatest challenge to you? If it is the former, how might you practice humility? Is it time to roll up your sleeves and engage in the hard labour of servanthood? It the latter proves more challenging, why not take time to reflect on the countless stories of unexpected victories that we find in the bible and throughout church history? Most of all, consider the cross where Christ's own humiliation laid the foundations for the salvation of creation.

Chapter Nine

God's Call to Us

THIS EXTRACT IS TAKEN FROM THE PROLOGUE OF
THE *RULE OF ST BENEDICT.*

Listen to the teacher's instructions, child; open your heart to them.
I tell you this as a father who loves you – hear me, and do what
I say! Obedient work will bring you back to him – you drifted
away from him by disobedient laziness. My message is for you,
then, if you are ready to surrender your own desires and fight
for the true king, Christ the Lord, with the strongest and glorious
weapons of obedience.

First, whenever you start something worthwhile, you must pray
insistently to him to complete it. He has already adopted us as
His children, so we should never do things which will make Him
regret this. We must always use the good things He has given us
obediently, so that He has no cause to turn into an angry father
who must disinherit his children, or a fearful Lord, enraged by
our sins, who will punish forever worthless servants who refuse
to follow Him to glory.

Up, then, finally! The Scripture calls us! 'It is time for us to rise
from our sleep,' it says [Rom. 13:11]. Let's open our eyes to God's
light, and our ears to the heavenly voice that keeps calling out 'if
you hear His voice today, do not harden your hearts' [Ps. 94:8].
And again: 'If you have ears to hear, listen to what the Spirit is
saying to the churches' [Rev. 2:7]. What does the Spirit say? 'Come,
children, listen to me: I will teach you the fear of God' [Ps. 33:12].
'Run while you have life's light, and the death's darkness will not
catch you' [Jn. 12:15].

God is looking for someone to serve Him. He calls out to a
crowd, 'Is there anyone here who longs for life, and wants to

see good days?' [Ps. 33:13]. If you hear God's voice, and you answer 'Me!', God says to you, 'If you long for true life, eternal life, then "Keep your tongue free from evil, and your lips from speaking lies; turn from evil and do good; seek peace – make it your goal"[Ps. 33:14–15]. When you have done this, "My eyes will be on you, and my ears will listen for your prayers, and before you ask, I will show myself to you"' [Ps. 33:16]. What could be better than God's voice calling to us like this, my friends? See how tenderly the Lord shows us the road to life! So let us clothe ourselves in faith and good works, and set out on the path, guided by the gospel, so that we may be found worthy to see God, who has called us into His kingdom.

Do you want to live in God's kingdom? We will never get there, unless we hurry to do good things! Ask the Lord, with the prophet, 'Lord, who can live in your tabernacle; who can dwell on your holy mountain?' [Ps. 14:1]. After asking the question, friends, we do well to listen to the Lord's answer, because he shows us the way to the tabernacle. He says 'Anyone who proceeds through life without any stain of evil, who behaves justly in everything, who speaks truth, even inwardly, who has never spoken deceitfully, who has never done evil to a neighbour, or even listened to snide gossip about someone else [Ps. 14:1–3]. Someone like this has defeated the enemy, the devil, at every turn, flinging him and his promptings far away. Someone like this seizes temptation when it is young, and smashes it against the rock that is Christ [Ps. 137:9]. Such people fear the Lord. They do not get excited by their own good deeds, because they realize that this is God's power, not their own efforts, that makes good things happen. So they praise the Lord for working in them, saying with the prophet 'Not to us, Lord, not to us, but to your name be glory!' [Ps. 113:9]. The apostle Paul refused to take credit for the power of his preaching. He said 'I am what I am by God's grace.' [1 Cor. 15:10] Again, he said 'Whoever boasts should boast in the Lord' [2 Cor. 10:17]. This is why the Lord says, in the gospel, 'If you hear these words of mine and live by them, you will be like someone wise, who builds a house on rock. When the floods rise, and the winds blow, they beat against that house, but it did not fall, because it was built on rock' [Mt. 7:24–25].

So the Lord waits for us to turn his holy words into actions every day. This is what we should do. Our days have been lengthened to give us the chance to repent and change our lives. The apostle tells us this: 'Do you not know that the patience of God is leading you to repentance?' [Rom. 2:4]. The Lord Himself assures us in His mercy: 'I do not desire the death of a sinner; I want them to turn to life' [Ezek. 33:11].

Friends, we have asked the Lord who may live in His tabernacle; we have heard the rules for living there. So we need to get ready for war – the war of holy obedience to God's laws. If we find something impossible by nature, we should ask the Lord to give us grace to make it possible for us. If we want to reach eternal life and avoid the pains of hell then – while there is time, while we are in this body, and can do these things – we must run, run now, and gain treasures that are eternal!

So we plan to create a school, a school for God's service. We hope that there will be nothing difficult in the way we have arranged it. We might sometimes be a little strict to make sure that lives are well lived and love is ever-present – that will be best for everyone involved. Do not let fear push you away from the road that leads to salvation! It is inevitably narrow to begin with, but as we travel along it our hearts will overflow with the inexpressible delights of His love, as we run in the way of God's commandments. So we will never turn from His commands, but follow them faithfully in the monastery until we die; we will patiently share in the suffering of Christ, so that we may also share His glory.

More to think and pray ...

1. The role of the prophet is usually an uncomfortable one. Having called his people to stand up for him, God often guarantees that their audience will not listen and that their message falls on stony ground. In what areas of our life is God calling us to the role of the prophet and, given what we have just said, what kind of response can we expect if we live up to this call?

2. Are there jobs that we have started for Jesus that are as yet uncompleted? Why is this? Is it because the work takes time or because our attention has wandered? Take a moment to pray for this unfinished business.

3. Could we do with a school for God's service? In what areas of life would we like to serve more effectively? Are there things we can do or stop doing in order to make this happen?

The Nicene Creed

We believe in one God,
the Father, the Almighty,
maker of heaven and earth,
of all that is, seen and unseen.

We believe in one Lord, Jesus Christ,
the only Son of God,
eternally begotten of the Father,
God from God, light from light,
true God from true God,
begotten, not made,
of one Being with the Father;
through him all things were made.
For us and for our salvation
he came down from heaven,
was incarnate of the Holy Spirit and the Virgin Mary
and became truly human.
For our sake he was crucified under Pontius Pilate;
he suffered death and was buried.
On the third day he rose again
in accordance with the Scriptures;
he ascended into heaven
and is seated at the right hand of the Father.
He will come again in glory to judge the living and the dead,
and his kingdom will have no end.

We believe in the Holy Spirit, the Lord, the giver of life,
who proceeds from the Father [and the Son],
who with the Father and the Son is worshipped and glorified,
who has spoken through the prophets.
We believe in one holy catholic and apostolic Church.
We acknowledge one baptism for the forgiveness of sins.
We look for the resurrection of the dead,
and the life of the world to come. AMEN.

Chapter Ten

Light and Learning

THE FOLLOWING TWO POEMS ARE BY MARIANNE FARNINGHAM AND WERE FIRST PUBLISHED IN 1866.

Let There Be Light

Now, as in thy voice of thunder
Thous didst cleave the chaos asunder,
Yet once more perform the wonder –
    Mightiest, give us light.

Now as comforts are declining,
In the darkness we are pining
For the radiance of thy shining –
    Father, give us light.

We our weary way are pressing
Over hills and steeps distressing;
Pray we for one precious blessing –
    Master, give us light.

We are thy displeasure winning,
We are ignorant and sinning,
For a better life's beginning –
    Holiest, give us light.

Grasping in the darkness, yearning
For a high and quick discerning
Of the truths we should be learning –
    Spirit, give us light.

In our thirst and hunger, needing
Pastures where thy lambs are feeding,
Listen to our earnest pleading –
    Jesus, give us light.

Near to thee we would be hiding,
In the night of love's providing,
To thy cross our worn feet guiding –
    Saviour, give us light.

Learn of Me

We would be children, Saviour, ever sitting at thy feet,
And learning of thy gracious lips the lessons that are meet,
And we would hush our trivial words, to hear what thou wilt say,
For, oh, we need thy holy love to help us every day.

Thou wert the ever patient one. We frown and fume and fret,
Beneath the ire and scorn of men we're ne'er contented yet.
We know not how to trust and wait, dear Saviour teach us how,
Breathe on us patience for our life, as near to thee we bow.

Thou wert the never-sinning one. We sin in word and thought,
Our every act is tainted, every deed with darkness fraught.
O Jesus, teach us how to live, that in the midst of sin
We yet may grow akin to thee, thy smile of love may win.

Thou wert the ever loving one. We only love in part,
For anger and impatience dwell in our divided heart;
And we are full of thoughts for self. A Saviour wilt thou be,
And Teacher till we shall have gained resemblance unto thee.

'Learn of me,' So we would, O Christ, but weak and tired we grow;
O teach us day by day to live within this world of woe;
And bring us in thine own good time to the better school above,
That we may sing the glad new song of all thy patient love.

More to think and pray ...

1. The God who speaks into being time and space and all that's within it is the same God who addresses us in Jesus. Reflect on what it means to have the creator of the universe as our teacher, friend and guide.

2. The second poem juxtaposes Christ's perfection with our fallenness and yet the poet is clear that failure is to be expected and not feared. Take time to thank God for the fact that he not only gives us permission to fail but turns these inglorious moments into object lessons in discipleship.

3. Finally, while failure is to be expected, Farningham still challenges us to imitate Christ in all we do. As we come to the end of this section, what have you learned about Christ and how might you become more like him?

SECTION TWO

✠

LIVING

Chapter Eleven

How to Keep a Broken Heart

THIS SERMON WAS PREACHED BY JOHN BUNYAN AND ORIGINALLY ENTITLED 'HOW TO KEEP THE HEART TENDER'.

While some try to mend a broken heart, the disciple knows how to keep it tender. But how do we achieve this? Before giving advice, I must offer several cautions.

Cautions:

- Stay vulnerable. Don't rush away from the convictions that bruised and broke your heart in the first place but rather remember and reflect on those things as you wait for the grace of God and the redeeming blood of Christ.

- Keep good company. Living with the wrong crowd stifles our convictions, kills our best desires and causes many to face the pain of judgement. If a friend does not help you in your walk with Christ then he or she is not your friend. Be wise in the friends you keep [Prov. 13:20].

- Watch your tongue. Be careful of idle talk, gossip and tittle tattle. Be quick to leave the room when foolishness, malice or obscenity, enter. Be warned, for foolish lips and a fast tongue will soon sell our soul before you know it. Cheap talk costs lives (Prov. 14:7; 18:7; 1 Cor. 15:33).

- The devil's in the detail. Beware of the smallest sin. Don't even think about it as it will only grow from there. Remember, King David's eye took his heart and then, from there, his lust led him to take the wife and the life of a friend. The first sin is only ever the thin edge of the wedge (Heb. 3:12, 13).

- Find good role models. Be careful who you follow and where they might lead. Don't follow anyone blindly for sometimes Satan uses the bad habits of godly people to lead disciples astray. In the same way, learn from the lives of godly people whose habits live up to God's word (Gal. 2:11–13).
- Keep believing. Take care not to foster doubt or allow unbelief to fester. Keep your head on heavenly things, on truth and reality. A heart cannot be tender if it has become hardened to God himself (Heb. 3:12).

Observing these cautions with care and diligence will help to keep our hearts open and available to God.

Advice

And now for some advice …

- Go deeper. Work hard to grow your knowledge of God and allow his presence to warm your heart. Labour after a deep knowledge of God's presence (Prov. 15:3), power (Heb. 1:11–12), justice (Heb. 12:19) and faithfulness (Mt. 5:18; 24:35).
- Seek to understand the nature of sin and the power of temptation. Having learned the nature of these soul destroying forces, guard yourselves against them in ever way possible. Remember that sin turns angels into devils, brings judgement down on anyone, expelled Adam and Eve from the garden, cost Christ his very life and created the pain of hell.
- Consider the fragile nature of our lives right now. Remind one another of the certainty of death and the uncertainty of its timing. Only God knows and determines the length of our life span. What's more, we have just one chance to live and die well. This life is no rehearsal (Heb. 9:27).
- Anticipate the day of judgement when Christ will sit on his throne, the trumpet will sound and the dead will be raised up. Imagine the moment when Christ shall separate men one from another and divide his sheep from those goats. Think about the opening of the Lamb's book of life and the event where all will be judged (Rev. 20:12, 15:2, 22:12).

- Remember that Jesus did not protect his own heart against sorrow or suffering; for this would have meant him hardening his heart against you and me. On the contrary, he awakened himself and opened his heart with great compassion. He clothed himself in grace and kindness and embraced us with his saving love. In him, heaven poured out every mercy.

- Hence, if we wish to stay tender and remain vulnerable before God and others we should above all think on Christ, and learn from his perfect example.

More to think and pray ...

1. What strategies do you employ to cover up your vulnerability? What are your favourite protection mechanisms? Reflect on how you might be more honest with yourself and others about your fragility and insecurity. Rest assured that your transparency will enable God to work in you and through you.

2. What details in your life hold you back from walking closer and further with Jesus? Share them with a fellow disciple and travelling companion and benefit from their care and support as you move forward.

3. How can you extend your knowledge of Jesus and thus deepen your devotion. Why not commit to reading a book about God that you would normally consider too heavy or far outside your normal range of reading? It may help to select one of the texts from which some of these extracts have been taken and work through this. If this appears daunting ask a friend to read along too. You could even start a *Walk This Way* book club!

Chapter Twelve

Prayer and Constancy

THESE POEMS ARE TAKEN FROM *THE TEMPLE*,
BY GEORGE HERBERT.

Prayer

Prayer the Church's banquet, Angel's age,
   God's breath in man returning to his birth,
   The soul in paraphrase, heart in pilgrimage,
The Christian plummet sounding heaven and earth;

Engine[1] against the Almighty, sinner's tower,
   Reversed thunder, Christ-side-piercing spear,
   The six-days world transposing in an hour,
A kind of tune, which all things hear and fear;

Softness, and peace, and joy, and love, and bliss,
   Exalted Manna, gladness of the best,
   Heaven in ordinary, man well dressed,
The Milky Way, the bird of Paradise,

      Church-bells beyond the stars heard, the souls blood,
      The land of spices; something understood.

Constancy

Who is the honest man?
He that doth still and strongly good pursue,

---

[1] i.e., a siege engine that allows a castle to be invaded.

To God, his neighbour, and himself most true:
     Whom neither force nor fawning can
Unpin, or wrench from giving all their due.

     Whose honesty is not
So loose or easy, that ruffling wind
Can blow away, or glittering look it blind:
     Who rides his sure and even trot,
While the world now rides by, now lags behind.

     Who, when great trials come,
Nor seeks, nor shuns them; but doth calmly stay,
Till he the thing and the example weigh:
     All being brought into a sum,
What place or person calls for, he doth pay.

     Whom none can work or woo
To use in anything a trick or sleight;
For above all things he abhors deceit:
     His words and works and fashion too
All of a piece, and all are clear and straight.

     Who never melts or thaws
At close temptations: when the day is done,
His goodness sets not, but in dark can run:
     The sun to others writeth laws,
And is their virtue; Virtue is his Sun.

     Who, when he is to treat
With sick folks, women, those whom passions sway,
Allows for that, and keeps his constant way:
     Whom others faults do not defeat;
But though men fail him, yet his part doth play.

     Whom nothing can procure,
When the wide world runs bias, from his will
To writhe his limbs, and share, not mend the ill,
     This is the Mark-man, safe and sure,
Who still is right, and prays to be so still.

More to think and pray ...

1. Which of Herbert's images for prayer do you find attractive?
2. ... And which seem strange or repellent to you? Why? Can you understand why he found them helpful?
3. What challenges you in Herbert's account of human constancy?

Wandering thoughts when praying

One thing that might well help with the problem of distracting thoughts while praying: often enough, you will suddenly remember or think of something you ought to do. This may be just because it happens to pop into your mind just then; it may be the prompting of God's Spirit; either way, it is in your head, and potentially distracting you from your prayers. Keep a notebook, or even a scrap of paper, and a pen handy whenever you pray; then you can make a note of whatever it is you think of, and leave it there to come back to after the time of prayer.

Chapter Thirteen

Royal Road and Holy Cross

THIS EXTRACT IS TAKEN FROM THE WRITINGS
OF THOMAS À KEMPIS.

1. 'Deny yourself, take up your cross, and follow me' [Mt. 16].
   Many people think this is a hard message. It will be much
   harder, though, to hear the final command 'Away from me,
   you who do evil, and into the eternal flames!' [Mt. 25]. Those
   who hear the message of the cross now, and follow it, need
   fear nothing then when they hear of the final condemnation.
   All will see the sign of the cross when the Lord comes as
   judge. So everyone who serves the cross, everyone who lived
   as Jesus the crucified lived, can come to Christ the judge full
   of confidence.

2. So why fear to take up the cross? This is the road to the
   kingdom! Safety, life, protection from enemies – all these are
   found in the cross! In the cross we can taste heaven's delights;
   in the cross our minds grow strong, our spirits become joyful,
   our virtues blossom and bloom. In the cross holiness becomes
   perfect. There is no health for the soul, and no hope of eternal
   life, except in the cross. So take up your cross! Follow Jesus!
   Then you will enter eternal life. He walked ahead of you,
   carrying His own cross, and died for you on that cross. You
   also ought to carry your cross, and aim to die on it. Because
   if you have died with Him, you will live with Him just the
   same way. And if you have shared His suffering, you will
   share His glory too.

3. The cross is everything! You have to die! There is no other way
   to life, no route to real peace of mind, except the road of the

holy cross, and daily dying to self. Go wherever you like; look for anything you like – you will not find a higher way above this one, or a safer way below it. The way of the holy cross is the only way! If you could arrange everything as seems best to you, you would still find that suffering would come, whether you wanted it or not. So you will always meet the cross. You will either find physical pain or spiritual disquiet wherever you look.

4. Sometimes God will withdraw for a while; sometimes other people will disturb you; more importantly, you will often be a burden to yourself! Nothing will heal, or even ease your pain – you must endure what God wills for you. Now, God wills that you should learn to meet troubles without help, so that you surrender yourself to Him completely, and learn humility from suffering. No-one really understands Christ's suffering except someone who has had to suffer the same way. The cross is always ready, it waits for you everywhere. You can't escape – wherever you go, it is still you who goes, and the cross is yours. Turn upwards or downwards, look within or outside – everywhere you meet the cross, and so you will always need patient endurance to have peace of mind, and to gain an eternal crown.

5. If you willingly carry your cross, it will carry you. It will lead you to the end you long for, where suffering will end, as is promised. But that is not in this world. If you carry your cross unwillingly, you make the suffering heavier and worse, but you can't not carry it. If you throw away one cross, there is no doubt that another will find you – and that one might be heavier.

6. Why do you try to escape suffering, when no-one has ever been able to avoid it? Which of the saints was ever without a cross and trouble? Jesus Christ our Lord, even, did not have one hour free of the anguish of His suffering. Scripture says it: 'Christ had to suffer, and to rise from the dead, and enter into His glory' [Lk. 24]. So will you look for a different road from this royal way, the way of the holy cross? The whole life of Christ was cross and martyrdom; would you seek for yourself rest and fun?

7. You are wrong, completely wrong, if you try to avoid trouble and suffering. Human life is full of difficulties at every turn, and surrounded by crosses. And the further you go in discipleship, the heavier the crosses will seem, because love feels the pain of exile more sharply! The pain of someone so troubled finds some relief, though, because they know that much good will come from suffering their cross.

8. When we submit to it willingly, every painful burden is transformed into faith in God's coming help. Even as suffering ravages our bodies, our spirits grow strong through God's grace. Sometimes someone will find such comfort in the middle of his pain and trouble, through embracing the cross of Christ, that they would not want to be without the difficulties and suffering, because they believe that God embraces them the more, the more they have had to suffer for Him. This is not our own strength, but Christ's grace, which works so powerfully in us that we can embrace and love the things that normally we would run away from.

9. By ourselves, we cannot bear the cross. We cannot love the cross, we cannot take control of our desires, renounce reputation, accept insults, forget ourselves and desire to be forgotten. We cannot cope with troubles and losses, and desire no riches in this world. In our own strength, we cannot do any of this – but if we trust in the Lord, we will be given strength from above, and the world and the flesh will be under our control. We will not even need to be afraid of the enemy, the Devil, if we have been armed with faith, and marked by the cross of Christ.

10. So be a good, a faithful servant of Christ! Put your shoulder to the cross of your Lord, who was crucified out of love for you. Get ready to face all sorts of troubles and difficulties in this poor life, because it will always be like that, wherever you go, however you try to hide. It has to be like this – there is no way of easing evil troubles and sorrows, save by bearing them. Drink the Lord's cup in love, if you want to be His friend and follower. Let God give you help as it pleases Him; you set yourself to face troubles, and think of them as the best help; for 'the sufferings of this time are not worth comparing

to the future glory to be won' – even if you alone had to bear them all.

11. When you get to the point where you can accept trouble with pleasure because of Christ, then you can think that you are in a good place – because there you have found heaven on earth. As long as trouble gets you down, and you try to escape it, then you will struggle, and trouble will follow you everywhere.

12. If you commit yourself to the task given to you, that is, to suffer and to die, you will soon be made better, and you will find peace. Even if you had been taken up to the third heaven with Paul, that would not free you from suffering. 'I will show you,' says Jesus Himself, 'what you must suffer for my name.' Therefore suffering is your lot in life, if you want to love Jesus and to serve him forever.

13. You should wish that you were worthy to suffer something for Jesus' name! Great glory would lie ahead of you, the saints in heaven would rejoice – and the people you know would be built up and encouraged. Everyone praises patience, but few are willing to suffer patiently. You should surely suffer a little for Christ, when so many suffer greatly for worldly things.

14. Know this for certain: you must die every day of your life. The more we die to self, the more we begin to live to God. No one can grasp divine truths unless they have resigned themselves to bear troubles for Christ. Nothing is more acceptable to God, nothing better for you in this world, than to suffer willingly for Christ. If you had the choice, you should ask to be allowed to suffer trouble for Christ, not to be given many gifts. Then you would be more like Christ, and you would share with all His saints, too. The only way we learn and go forward is by bearing great troubles and difficulties.

15. If there had been anything better for us, more useful to our salvation, than suffering, then there is no doubt that Christ would have shown it to us in His words and actions. But He tells His first disciples, and everyone who wants to follow Him, to carry the cross. He says 'If you want to come after me, forget yourself, pick up your cross, and follow me.' So

when everything has been studied, this is the truth: 'we only enter the Kingdom of God through many troubles'.

More to think and pray ...

1. What fears or concerns hold you back in your walk with Jesus? It is helpful to think through and confess these things. Remember that Christ's perfect love casts out all fear and take time to list your worries in prayer. It may help to write them down. Ask God to take these away so that you can follow where Jesus is leading you next.

2. In a culture driven by consumption, sacrifice often seems a foreign, unattractive and even irrational activity. That said, the people of God throughout history have considered it an essential part of their faith and commitment. Are there aspects of our modern life that we could usefully sacrifice? Could we suspend a weekly activity for a period of regular study or prayer? Might we consider removing an item from our budget that we have too readily considered an essential when it is really a luxury? How might we re-employ those resources?

3. Again, in a world that avoids suffering at almost any cost how might we better identify with the Passion of Christ. Consider taking time to stand alongside and serve those that you know who are suffering. Be prepared to walk with them as they negotiate the road ahead. Rest assured that in sharing their trials you will see Jesus more clearly and share him more powerfully.

The Bible

'Teach me thy way, O Lord: and lead me in the right way, because of mine enemies.'

Psalm 27:13

Chapter Fourteen

God's Presence for Us

THIS EXTRACT WAS TAKEN FROM BROTHER
LAWRENCE'S *SPIRITUAL MAXIMS*.

'The Presence of God'

1. What do I mean by 'the presence of God'? I mean focusing ourselves on God, remembering that God is present. Sometimes we just know this; sometimes we have to believe it, and live as if we felt it.

2. I know someone who has been giving himself to the practice of the presence of God for forty years now.[1] He has many different words for it: sometimes has says it is simply something he does, at other times a clear and distinct knowledge of God; again, it might be an unclear sight, or a loving gaze, or just remembering God. Again, he calls it waiting on God, silent conversation with Him, confidence in God who gives us life and peace. He tells me, though, that all these different ways of talking about God's presence refer to the same thing, and that God is easily present to him.

3. How did he attain this state? By constant action, and often calling himself back to God's presence, it has become a way of life. Now, as soon as he is released from his work – and often even when he is in the middle of it – he rises above earthly things, and fixes his thoughts and attention and desire even on God. This has become a habit – it happens now without any

[1] Like Paul in 2 Corinthians, Brother Lawrence is describing his own religious experience but putting it in the mouth of another.

effort on his part. God is the centre of his life, his resting place. At these moments, he is always filled with faith and joy; this is what he calls the 'actual' presence of God – all the other things I have mentioned are summed up in this. He feels that there is only him and God in the world, and talks constantly with God, asking for whatever he needs, and endlessly rejoicing with God in a million different ways.

4. We should note, however, that this conversation with God happens deep in his heart – in the deepest place, indeed. Only there can we speak to God face to face. When we do, we know the peace that is beyond understanding, and the troubles of this world mean almost nothing to us, and hardly ever intrude on the peace within.

5. This sweet loving sight of God begins a fire in the heart, a divine fire which quietly burns within us. When this fire burns, our hearts grasp hold of the love of God so strongly that we actually have to disguise the strength of our love of God when with others!

6. We would be astonished to discover what goes on between God and the heart at these times. God delights so much in this relationship that he allows anything to the heart that desires to live forever with him. It is almost as if God fears that the heart will turn again to earthly things, and so He makes it His business to give that heart whatever it might want, fills it with such wonderfully good things that it could not even think to want otherwise. All this happens without any effort on our part – we only have to accept what God gives.

7. God's presence is our life and our food, which we can gain by the Lord's grace in the way I will now explain:

The Way to Discover God's Presence

1. The first thing we need is a truly pure life.
2. The second is to be committed to practicing God's presence. We need to keep our inward gaze fixed faithfully on God. We should do this calmly; humbly; lovingly – and we should not be distracted from it by anything.

3. Look to God, even if it is only for a moment, before beginning anything. Look to Him from time to time while you are busy with it, and again when you finish. It will take time and a lot of practice for this to become second nature for you, so don't be discouraged if you fail often. This habit is a difficult one to acquire, it really is – but if you once get hold of it, joy will be your constant companion! ...

4. If you want to begin this way of life, I suggest you pray briefly, something like this: 'My God, I am completely yours.' Or, 'God of love, I love you with all my heart.' Or, 'Lord, make my heart like your heart.' Or some other words which love suggest to you. But be careful – there is nothing so deceitful as the human heart! You will find yourself quietly returning to the world. Fix yourself on God, on God alone! Force yourself to live in God's presence!

5. Living in God's presence is hard at first, but if you try and keep trying, your heart will be changed in amazing ways, without you even realizing it. You will discover so many of God's gifts, and quietly begin to gaze lovingly on God all the time. This is the holiest way of prayer – it is also the best, the easiest, the most powerful!

More to think and pray ...

1. Practise the presence of God. It is never a question of whether God turns up when we ask him or address him. His omnipresence means that he is always there. Hence the real question is whether we notice his presence and hear his voice. God is great at being in our presence but sadly we are often not so good at being in his! Take time and practise.

2. Know how you work. In the same way that we are all different, we all have different ways in which we most fruitfully encounter God. Write down the ways and means by which you have most regularly encountered him. Do you find it easy to meet Jesus as you meditate on scripture, pray as you walk, sit in a church, share with a friend, listen to music, wander through an art gallery, walk the dog, go for a run, etc.? Can you carve a regular time to meet God through one of these activities?

3. While all of us have our more natural ways of engaging with
   God, our prayer lives can also suffer from an attack of the
   same old, same old! Why not try something very different.
   Step outside of the comfort zone of your tradition or church-
   manship. Get thee to a monastery for a short retreat, attend a
   weekly church service in a very different congregation, plan a
   pilgrimage with friends, etc. Although Jesus travels with us in
   the ordinary ways, he also longs to reveal himself in out of the
   ordinary ways.

Meditation

Meditation is a word with a long history in Christian
discipleship, and we should not be scared into thinking
the idea is something weird brought to our world by the
fashionable faux Buddhism of the 1960s. At heart, it just
means thinking about something. Puritan writers would
suggest meditating on texts of Scripture by thinking how the
best preacher you know would unpack and apply the text to
your life; the medieval devotional writers sometimes stressed
meditation as a way to feel, rather than just know, truths: we
know that God is loving, but by meditating on that truth, by
thinking seriously about what it means and all the evidence
we have of it, we can begin to enjoy God's love and be
motivated by it, rather than just accepting it intellectually.

Chapter Fifteen

Money, Money, Money

FROM A SERMON ENTITLED 'THE USE OF MONEY', PREACHED BY JOHN WESLEY IN 1872 ON THE PARABLE OF THE TALENTS (LUKE 16:1–15).

This parable is filled with wisdom for Christians everywhere. While men of the world talk much about money, the subject is not sufficiently discussed by those called to stand out from the world. Having not learned how best to use this amazing resource, many Christians have failed to witness its true potential and power. Others, poets, prophets and preachers from almost every age, have railed against its corrupting tendencies and destructive possibilities. . . . But isn't this simply a predictable and empty rant? Are there good reasons for such judgement to sweep? No, not at all! It is the love of money that forms the root of all evil not the coins and the notes themselves. It is not money that is the problem but what we do with it. It can be used well and it can be used for ill, for the greatest good and the worst possible cause . . .

For the disciple, money is a gift from God. In the hands of God's people it feeds the starving, quenches the thirsty, clothes the naked and protects the vulnerable. Money can support a grieving widow and sustain a fatherless child. It can bring healing to the sick, ease to the suffering, sight to the blind and feet to the lame. In short, it can be the difference between life and death. As a result, disciples should learn how to use this valuable resource. We must teach and be taught how to invest money for the most glorious returns.

The first lesson is this: *make as much money as you can!* A disciple should make as much money as they can but this is not without certain sacred provisos. Firstly, we should be shrewd and fair in what we buy and how much we charge. We should never make money at the expense of our own health or at the cost of another's life. No investment, no matter how profitable, should be considered if it would damage our health or threaten the lives of others.... Whenever we discover a profession or industry which destroys the lives of its workers or customers, we should remind ourselves that 'life [is] more than food and the body more than clothing' (Mt. 6:25, NKJV). If we are already involved or invested in such a scheme we should get out immediately.

Secondly, the disciple must keep a good eye and healthy mind on their investments. Either by the Law of God or the law of the land, we should put no time or money into dubious deals or unlawful transactions. We must remember that theft is theft, whether from an individual or society, our neighbour or the taxman. Likewise, it is our sacred duty to avoid any business which has no regard for ethics, leads us or others into temptation or damages our soul by sucking the life from them. However, in the end it becomes impossible for one disciple to discern all these things for another so every Christian must make judgement for themselves.

Thirdly, disciples should make all they can without hurting their neighbours. If we love others as we love ourselves there should be no problem here. It is impossible to love someone while profiting from their poverty. We cannot care for someone while invading their lands, destroying their environment, demanding punishing payments on their loans or ignoring their oppression. Neither can we claim to love someone if our business practices drive them under or our purchases fail to provide fair payment for their labour. Swallowing gains at the cost of our neighbour will lead to us tasting hell!

The second lesson is this: *save all you can!* Having made all we can we should be prudent with the resources God gives us. Throwing money at unnecessary luxuries and unjustified expenses is like throwing God's gifts into the sea. Likewise, our expenditure should not be dictated by personal pleasure or an envious eye. Don't waste money on self-gratification. Despise delicacy and rest content with simplicity. Don't waste time and money on fancy clothes, needless ornaments or useless gadgets. Deny the vain temptation to spend money on personal pride or public perception. Don't spend to impress, hoping that others will notice your elegance, generosity or hospitality. Rather be content with the honour that comes from God.

Also, be careful not to throw money at your children for in doing so you will buy things that they certainly do not need. Gifting them with greed, selfishness and ingratitude is hardly the act of a kind and loving parent. Instead teach them, to take joy in simplicity and thank God that their needs have been met. Likewise, if you believe they will squander their inheritance then do not curse them further by leaving your money with them when you die.

The third lesson is this: *give all you can!* Making and saving money means nothing if we stop there. There is no point making money if you make nothing of it. Likewise, no money has been saved if we simply store it up. In either case you might as well throw it in the sea or bury it in the ground. Since he first made us the creator of the heavens and the earth has urged us to make something of our lives and the world that he has given. We are his trusted partners for one short season. Along with all we own and possess, we belong to him and we are to present all of this as a sacrifice to him through Jesus. In response he promises to reward this light and easy service with the eternal return of his glory.

Finally, if you wish to be a wise investor of all that God has given you follow these four simple steps. First, live according to your basic needs; buy food to eat, clothes to wear and whatever else you need for a healthy lifestyle. Secondly, ensure that your family is taken care of similarly. Thirdly, ensure that those you share your life with also have enough. Fourthly, make your surplus into good news for all men, sharing freely with those who have need, wherever you find them. If doubts remain as to how we spend our money, we should make these decisions the subject of prayer. Above and beyond all we must remember the keys to Christian prudence. Make all you can. Save all you can. Give all you can.

Brothers and Sisters we must live as wise and faithful stewards, using all that the good Lord gives to do good for our Lord. This is no small part of Christian life. Disciples must give all that they have and all that they are to the Father who gave every breath and bone of his only Son for them. In this, they are 'storing up for themselves a good foundation for the time to come, that they may hold of eternal life' (1 Tim. 6:19).

More to think and pray ...

1. Think about how you spend your resources and invest your savings. Do your financial commitments back up your faith in Christ and commitment to the truth and justice of his kingdom? Do you profit from the poverty of others? Do you always go for the cheapest goods rather than the most fairly traded products? If you passed your bank statement to your brother or sister what might they think? If you're not sure, you could always try it!

2. How might you better use the resources that God shares with you? How tempted are you to buy on impulse? Are there purchases which have become second nature that you could do without? How about doing Lent every month or fasting from certain spending for a year?

3. Take time to audit your own generosity. Removing the times when you give to others in order to appear generous or win their approval, how often do you lavish blessing on others? Why not regularly commit to impulsive acts of kindness and anonymous acts of generosity?

Chapter Sixteen

Cooks and Quartermasters

THIS EXTRACT IS TAKEN FROM *ST BENEDICT'S RULE*.

Quartermasters

When you have to choose someone to look after the community's supplies, find someone who is wise, who acts maturely, who is moderate in habits and not greedy with food. He should not be proud, or easily excited, not offensive or lazy, not wasteful. You want someone who fears God, who is like a father to the whole community. He will be careful in everything, and do nothing without instruction from the Abbot. He should be careful about such instructions. He should not annoy the other brothers. If someone happens to ask something from him inappropriately, he should not reject the demand haughtily – this will cause distress. Instead, he should deny the improper request humbly, giving good reasons. He should watch his own life, always remembering the Apostle's words: 'whoever serves well secures a good place for himself' [1 Tim. 3:3].

He should have a particular concern for the sick, for children, for guests, and for poor people. There is no doubt that he will be held accountable for these people on the day of judgement. He will view the monastery's crockery and goods just as if they were communion plate, and the bread and wine on the altar, and will be as careful and respectful with the least things as he would with these, the noblest. He should not be greedy, or wasteful or over-generous with the monastery's possessions. He should do everything carefully, and according to the abbot's orders.

Most of all, he must be humble! If there is nothing in the stores when something is asked for, he should give a kind word instead – it is written, 'A good word is better than the best gift' [Eccl. 18:17]. He must be careful with whatever the abbot trusts to him, and must not presume to do things the abbot has forbidden. He will provide the monks with their rations without either pride or delay – if he does not, they may be led astray, and remember what Scripture says about the person who 'leads one of the little ones astray' [Mt. 18:6]!

If the community is fairly large, he will need helpers, so that with their aid he can calmly do what he has to do. Requests should be made, and things given, at the proper times so that nothing will disturb or upset the house of God.

Kitchen helpers

Monks should serve each other. No-one will be let off kitchen duty, then, unless he is sick or busy with a significant task. Helping in the kitchen will lead to reward, and will increase our love. Give help to the less able, so that they can still serve in turn without any distress, and make sure everyone gets help, as far as the number of monks or local situation makes it possible. In a large community, the quartermaster should be excused kitchen duty – and we have said that those who are involved in important business should; but let everyone else serve one another in love.

On Saturday, the brother who is coming off duty should wash the towels which the monks use to wipe their hands and feet. He should wash everyone's feet, with the help of the brother who is next to serve. All the crockery should be washed and given to the quartermaster, who will hand it on to the next to serve. That way, the quartermaster will always know what he has given out, and what has come back.

Give the kitchen helpers something to drink and some bread an hour before the meal. (This is in addition to their normal rations.) That way, they can serve everyone else without suffering or complaining. On holy days, however, they should wait until the meal is over.

On Sunday those finishing their service and those beginning should bow before the others immediately after the morning service, and ask for their prayers. The helper who has finished his week should recite this verse of Scripture: 'Blessed are you, Lord God, for you given me help and comfort' [Ps. 86:17]. He should say this three times, and then receive a blessing. Then the one replacing him should say 'God come to my aid; Lord, hurry to help me' [Ps. 70:1]. Everyone should say this three times, then he also is blessed, and begins his service.

More to think and pray ...

1. Benedict spends much time discussing the right way to perform the role of 'quartermaster' in the monastery. How much of this might apply to your daily tasks? What would be different for you?
2. The servers in the monastery kitchens worked hard, but were needed to keep the community going. Are there ideas here that might help your church community?

Ellen Sturgis Hooper (1816–41)

'I slept, and dreamed that life was beauty;
I woke and found that life was duty.'

Beauty and Duty (1840)

Chapter Seventeen

Desert Fathers

THIS EXTRACT WAS TAKEN FROM THE WRITINGS OF
THE DESERT FATHERS.

One who was devoted to hard work saw someone carrying a dead man on a bier. He said to him, 'Are you carrying the dead? Go and carry the living!'

✠

It is said that one day some philosophers came to test the monks. One of the monks passed by in beautiful clothes, and they said, 'Come here!' but he angrily scorned them. Another monk, a big Libyan, went past, and they said to him, 'Hey, you, you old scoundrel of a monk, come here!' They forced him to come, and then they beat him, but he offered them the other cheek. Then they got up and bowed down before him, saying, 'Truly, this is a monk!' Then they sat him down in the middle of them and asked, 'What do you do in the desert that is more than we do? You fast – we also fast; you keep vigils – we also keep vigils; whatever you do, we do also! What do you do here in the desert that we do not do?'

The Father said to them, 'We – we hope in the grace of God, and we watch our thoughts.' They said to him, 'We can't do this!' And taught by this, they went away.

✠

A Father said, 'If someone asks something of you, even if it hurts you to give it to them, you need to take pleasure in the gift. It is written, after all, "If someone forces you to go a mile, go two miles with them." This means, if someone asks something of you, give it to him with your whole heart.'

✝

They tell of a brother who had made some baskets, and was putting the handles on when he heard his neighbour saying, 'What can I do? Market day is soon, and I have no handles to put on my baskets.' So he took the handles off his own baskets and took them to his brother, saying, 'I have these handles spare; take them, and put them on your own baskets.' So he made his brother's work succeed by neglecting his own.

✝

Three brothers went to the harvest one day, and agreed to work together. On the very first day, however, one of them fell ill and returned to his cell. One of others said to the last, 'Brother, you can see that our brother is ill; work a little harder, and I will do the same, and, trusting in God and helped by his prayers, I am sure we will be able to harvest his share.'

When the harvest was in, they came to receive their wages. They called the brother, and said to him, come, receive your wages brother!' But he said, 'What wage should I receive, seeing as I have harvested nothing?' They said, 'Because of your prayers, the harvest is in. Come, then, and receive your wages.' The argument went on and on, the first brother saying he deserved nothing, the others insisting that he take a wage.

Eventually, they went to see a great Father, and asked him to judge their case. 'Father,' the brother said to him, 'the three of us went harvesting. On the way to the fields that day, I became unwell, and returned to my cell. I had not harvested a single stalk, but my brothers are trying to force me, saying "Come, receive the wage for the work you have not done". However, the two others said, 'Father, the three of us were given work – we were given sixty acres to harvest. If we had not been three, we would not have finished, but because of our brother's prayers, we were enabled to finish the harvest quickly. So, we said to him, "take your wage," but he refuses to do so.'

When he heard this story, the Father was filled with wonder, and sent a follower to summon all the brothers. When they were all gathered, he said to them, 'Come, brothers, and hear just judgement given today!' Then the Father told them the whole story, and they together judged that the brother should receive his wage and do whatever he wanted to with it.

The brother left, weeping in sorrow.

More to think and pray ...

1. Can you watch your thoughts?
2. Did the Father in the last story judge rightly, do you think?
3. How easy do you find it to give things away when someone else's need is greater than yours?

Hartley Coleridge (1796–1849)

'But what is Freedom? Righty understood, a universal license to be good.'

'Liberty' (1833)

Chapter Eighteen

From Mourning to Joy

THIS EXTRACT IS TAKEN FROM *REVELATIONS OF DIVINE LOVE*, BY MOTHER JULIAN OF NORWICH.

Our generous Lord showed me the moaning and the mourning of the heart. He said this: 'I know, I really do, that you want to live for me cheerfully, gladly suffering whatever comes to you. And I know that out of love for me you are willing to suffer all the woe, the troubles and the distress that might come because you cannot live without sin. This is true, but do not be too upset about the sins you commit unwillingly.'

I understood from this that the Lord views His servants with pity, not with blame. In this passing life, we cannot live entirely without blame and sin. He loves us endlessly; we sin habitually; and He gently shows us our failings. When He does, we feel sorry, and we mourn appropriately, thinking about His mercy and clinging to His love and goodness. He is our medicine; we know that we do nothing but sin.

We gain humility from seeing our sin, and we realize again His everlasting love, and begin to thank and praise Him for that again. All this pleases Him. 'I love you,' He says, 'and you love me; our love will not be torn apart! So I suffer so that you can gain.' I saw all this in thinking about those wonderful words, 'I will keep you completely safe.'

I saw that our Blessed Lord longed for us to live in joy and longing for Him – all this lesson of love showed me that! And so I realized that anything harmful to us does not come from God, but from the enemy. God wants us to see this, as He shows us it in the sweet and gracious light of His kind love. Perhaps there is someone on earth who loves God like this and who God prevents from ever falling from this love – I don't know; God did not show that to me – but this is what He did show me: when we fall, and when we get up again, we are always, every moment, protected by God's tender love. The way God sees us, we never fail; the way we see ourselves, we never do anything but fail. Both these are true, but our Lord God's view is the highest truth. Praise be to God for showing us this truth in this earthly life!

I realized that we need to see both these truths at once in this life. Seeing as God sees gives us spiritual comfort, and helps us to feel joy in God as we should; seeing in a human way keeps us in awe, and makes us feel our own shame. But God, our good Lord, wants us to see much more in His way, without forgetting the other, until we are raised up above, when we shall have the Lord Jesus as our reward, and be fulfilled and filled with eternal joy and happiness.

More to think and pray ...

1. 'The Lord views His servants with pity, not with blame.' Do you think this is true? How does it make you feel?
2. How easy do you find it to feel joy in God?
3. Do you think it is important to feel shame?

Roger Ascham (1515–68)

'I said ... how, and why, young children, were sooner allured by love, than driven by beating to attain good learning.'

The Schoolmaster (1570), Preface

'There is no such whetstone, to sharpen a good wit and encourage a will to learning, as is praise.'

The Schoolmaster (1570), bk. 1

Chapter Nineteen

Living for Others

THIS EXTRACT WAS TAKEN FROM THE WRITINGS OF
THE DESERT FATHERS.

A monk questioned a Father. He said 'Imagine two brothers – one lives alone in his cell six days every week, choosing devotions that are very painful. The other serves people who are sick. Whose work will God accept more readily?'

The Father said, 'Even if the brother who is alone for six days were to hang himself up by his nostrils, he could not equal the one who serves the sick!'

✠

Once Abbot John was climbing up from Scetis with some other monks, and the one who was leading them took a wrong turning, because it was dark. The brothers said to Abbot John, 'What should we do, Father? The brother has got the path wrong, and we might become lost and die!'

That old man said, 'If we say anything to him, he might be hurt and ashamed. Instead, I will pretend to be worn out, and say I cannot walk any further. And I will say that I must rest here till morning.'

He did this, and the others said 'We will not go any further, then, but will sit here with you.' And they sat there till morning, rather than offending their brother.

✠

They told of Abbot Gelasius, who had a book, made of parchment, worth forty or fifty thousand pounds. The whole of the Old and New Testaments were written in it. It was placed in the church, where anyone could read it if they wanted to. A wandering monk came and attached himself to the old man. When he saw the book he was overcome with desire for it and stole it. Then he came out and left. The old man did not chase him to arrest him, although he knew what he had done.

The monk went to the city, and looked for someone to sell the book to. When he found someone willing to buy it, he asked for thirty-five thousand. But his buyer wanted to assess it, and said 'Give it to me first so I can show it to someone, then I will pay you.'

The monk gave him the book, and he took it to Abbot Gelasius for valuing. The old man said, 'Buy it – it is an excellent book, and worth the money.'

When he got back, though, the buyer lied and did not tell the monk what the old man had said. 'I showed the book to Abbot Gelasius,' he said, 'and he told me that it was overpriced and not worth what you said.'

When he heard this, the monk said 'Did the old man say nothing else to you?'

'Nothing,' came the reply.

Then the brother said, 'I don't want to sell anymore.' He was convicted of his fault, and he went to the old man and repented. He asked him to take the book back, but the old man would not. Then the brother said to him, 'If you will not take it, I will never know peace again!'

The old man said to him, 'If you really cannot be at peace, then I will take it.' And that brother remained with him until he died, benefiting from the old man's patience.

More to think and pray …

1. Is service to those in need really more important than devotion, as the first story suggests?
2. Is lying to prevent hurt to a sister or brother a good thing to do?

3. Abbot Gelasius seems to not want to own his valuable book; can you understand his reaction, or is it just strange?

Fëdor Dostoevsky

'I ask myself: "What is hell?" and I answer thus: "The suffering of being no longer able to love".'

The Brothers Karamazov bk. 2 ch. 6

Chapter Twenty

Soul Poetry

THESE EXTRACTS ARE TAKEN FROM A COLLECTION
OF POETRY BY MARIANNE FARNINGHAM, ENTITLED
LYRICS OF THE SOUL.

Teach Us To Love

Lord, teach us how to love
    After Thine own great way;
So much of self is in our love,
    Deliver us, we pray.

Our hearts are cold and hard,
    So little are we moved,
And yet we should know how to love
    For we Thy love have proved.

Give us the light and glow
    The passion and the power;
Send the warm springtide to our hearts
    To consecrate love's hour.

O Lord, whose wondrous love
    Allured Thee from above,
Quicken our hearts for Thy dear sake,
    And teach us how to love.

The Wider Outlook

Be not too narrow in thy aim,
A large-spaced world is thine to claim;
Believe that greatest things are wrought
By broadened love and generous thought.

Go not in cynic mood to meet
Thy brother in the crowded street;
Canst thou not hope for all men see?
Christ died for them who died for thee.

Keep clear swift eyes to note the good
That dwells in all the brotherhood,
Nor judge that they must needs be wrong
Who cannot sing thy favourite song.

God's love is stronger than we deem,
His heaven is larger than our dream,
And Christ who died for love of men
Can bring the wanderers home again.

For Whom Christ Died

He is about you everywhere;
Perhaps he is your cross, or care,
He needs your pity and your prayer
        For whom Christ died.

He walks life's ways with weary feet,
He faces you where crossroads meet –
Without Him is your Heaven complete?
        For whom Christ died?

You turn to him unpitying eyes
Because he is not strong or wise:
He is the man whom you despise
        For whom Christ died.

Much wrong and evil has he done,
He does not know himself God's son,

He does not dream *he* is the one
For whom Christ died.

But unto you it is revealed;
Then stand beside him on the field,
And hearten him, lest he should yield,
For whom Christ died.

His heart is sad, his eyes are dim,
Fill up his joy-cup to the brim.
Be brave, and true, and strong for him
For whom Christ died.

More to think and pray ...

1. Take time to reflect and pray on how Christ's love might better permeate your life today.
2. Note down a number of miracles that you hoped would happen but have given up praying for. Give them again to God in prayer knowing that he can do immeasurably more than you expect or imagine.
3. Take time to pray for people that you will see and meet this week. Before you make any request, thank Jesus for dying for them and allow this world changing truth to shape your intercession.

SECTION THREE

✠

GROWING

Chapter Twenty-one

Renewing Devotion

THIS EXTRACT IS FROM THE *IMITATION OF CHRIST* BY THOMAS À KEMPIS.

1. The best religious life is full of virtues, so that we are on the inside what we appear to be on the outside. Actually, we should be better inside than out, because God examines our hearts, and we should honour God above all, wherever we may be, and walk purely in his sight, as the angels do. We need to renew our commitment every day, to stir ourselves up to care about holiness, as if today was the first day of our Christian lives. We should say, 'Help me, Lord God, to be committed and active in your holy service, and grant me today – right now – a new beginning, because what I have done so far is nothing.'

2. We will grow as fast as we commit ourselves to grow. Whoever wants to make quick progress needs to be very committed and diligent. But if someone who is seriously committed often drops short, what will it be like for someone of weaker or less common commitment? We lose our commitment for all sorts of reasons – the least failure in our own devotional rule will almost always bring some loss. But our commitment depends on the grace of God, not on our own ideas – we should hand everything over to God, because 'man proposes, but God disposes' (Prov. 16), and our paths are not our own.

3. If you sometimes lay aside your rule out of pity, or to do good for someone else, you will find it easy to pick it up later. But if you carelessly drop it out of negligence, or because you are tired or bored, you deserve to be blamed, and you will feel the hurt. However hard we try, we will still find that we fail to some

extent in many ways. But we must make certain resolutions and commit ourselves to them, especially against those things that damage us the most. We should examine and discipline our lives and our thoughts, because both contribute to our progress.

4. If you can't examine yourself constantly, then do it from time to time – at least twice a day, morning and evening. In the morning make your resolutions, and in the evening examine your behaviour. How were you today in thought, word and deed? These are the areas where you have most likely offended against God and neighbour. Prepare yourself to face the devil's evils; control your gluttony, and you will find it easier to control every desire of the flesh. Never be completely idle – but be reading or writing or praying or meditating or doing something useful for the common good. However physical disciplines should be undertaken carefully – they are not equally suited to all.

5. Whatever is not communal should not be shown in public, for private duties are best carried out in secret. Be careful not to be lazy about public duty, and more ready to do what is private. When you have done everything fully and faithfully, if there is more time, allow yourself to follow where devotion will lead you. The same devotional practice will not work for everyone – one suits one person better; another, another. Devotional practices even vary according to times – some are best for festivals, and some for ordinary days; we need some when we face temptation, and others when we enjoy peace and tranquillity; some help us when we are sad, others when we 'rejoice in the Lord'.

6. We should renew our devotion around the time of the great festivals. We should re-commit ourselves from festival to festival, as if we were about to leave this world and join the great heavenly feast. So we should prepare ourselves more earnestly in devotional times, and live more devoutly, and more strictly observe our rules, as if we were about to receive from God the reward of our work.

7. If this is deferred, we should believe that we are not yet ready, unworthy of such great glory. It will be revealed to us at the

right time, the time God has set, and we should be zealous in getting ready for this. 'Blessed is the servant,' as Luke's Gospel says, 'who, when the Lord comes, is found watching. Truly I tell you, he will place him over all he has.'

More to think and pray ...

1. Follow Thomas' advice and pray his own prayer: 'Help me, Lord God, to be committed and active in your holy service, and grant me today – right now – a new beginning, because what I have done so far is nothing.'
2. Take time to review your discipleship over the past day or week. If you had this time over again, what might you change about your behaviour or attitude?
3. 'Look busy, Jesus is coming!' Assuming that the popular car bumper sticker is not the end of all wisdom in this regard, how might we prepare for an encounter with Jesus? If Jesus was coming to your place of work or residence tomorrow, how might you prepare? Now remember, that Jesus will be joining you wherever you go tomorrow.

Herbert Agar (1897–1980)

'The truth which makes men free is for the most part the truth which men prefer not to hear.'

A Time for Greatness (1942), ch. 7

Chapter Twenty-two

Love Alone

THIS EXTRACT HAS BEEN TAKEN FROM THE 'CONVERSATIONS OF BROTHER LAWRENCE'.

Brother Lawrence said that love alone drove him, not what he could get out of life, and not even a desire to be saved rather than damned. Deciding to make the love of God the aim of everything he did was the best thing he had ever done. He was pleased if he could pick up a bit of grass from the floor for the love of God, seeking him alone and nothing else – not even his gifts.

Behaving like this will inevitably lead to God giving of His infinite grace. But when we receive the benefits of His grace, the love that it produces, we must not become too excited by this – it is not God, and we know and believe that He is infinitely better than anything else we might experience. If we act like this, there will be a strange battle between God and the soul: God giving, and the soul disclaiming what it receives from God. In this struggle, the soul is by faith as strong as God – stronger even – because He can never give so much that the soul cannot renounce what He gives.

We should not be satisfied with gifts of ecstasy and rapture; instead we should put such things behind us and seek God beyond His gifts. If such things come, however, we should not pause to enjoy them; God is still what matters.

God will repay promptly and lavishly everything we do for Him. Brother Lawrence said that at times he wanted to be able to hide from God so that his love might receive no reward. He wanted to be able to do something purely for God.

Brother Lawrence said that he once had a terrible spiritual trouble, because he believed he was inevitably damned. Nobody could have convinced him otherwise, but he had eventually thought about it in this way: 'I came to the spiritual life for one reason only: the love of God, and I have tried to live only for Him. Whether I am lost or saved, I want to live constantly only out of pure love for Him. I shall have this good at least: until I die, I shall have done everything I can to love Him.' This trouble lasted four years, and he suffered seriously because of it.

Since that time, he said that he had not thought about either heaven or hell. His life has been perfect freedom and constant joy. He puts his sins before God, as if to tell God that he does not deserve His help, but this has not stopped God from filling and satisfying him. Sometimes it is as if God holds him up before the whole host of heaven, so that they may see how gracious He is in pouring out His goodness on such a miserable sinner.

He told me that we need to work fairly hard to begin to form a habit of talking constantly with God, and giving Him everything we do, but after a little effort we would find that His love rousing us to it with no difficulty.

He expected that, after God had given him so many happy days, his share of trouble and suffering would come. This did not worry him, as he knew that he could do nothing himself, but God would give him the strength to cope.

He always spoke to God when a chance of doing something good came along, saying 'My God, I cannot do this unless you help me.' Then he received more than enough strength.

Whenever he failed, he did nothing but confess his fault, saying to God 'I would never do anything else if you left me alone. You must prevent me from falling and make good whatever is wrong.' After this, he didn't worry about his failure any more.

We ought to behave honestly and openly before God, speaking frankly to Him, and asking His help in everything as it happens to us. God never fails to help – Brother Lawrence's own life was the proof of this.

Recently, he had been sent to Burgundy to buy some wine for the monastery. He did not want to do this, because he had no business sense, and because he was disabled, and could not get about on the boat except by rolling over the barrels. He did not worry about this, however, or about buying the wine. He said to God that this was His business; afterwards he found that he had done well. Last year he was sent to the Auvergne on the same business; he could not tell at the time what sort of bargain he had got, but it later proved to be a good one.

It was the same with his work in the kitchen. He really did not like it, but he taught himself to do everything there for the love of God, and he asked God for help to do his work well at every turn. He had worked there for fifteen years, and found everything easy during that time.

His current job was much more to his taste, but he was as ready to leave it as he had been the previous one, because wherever he was he found fulfilment in doing every little thing out of love for God.

The set times of prayer in the monastery were no different for him than the rest of the day. He took retreats when told to by his spiritual director, but he did not particularly want or ask for them, because the hardest work could not turn his mind from God.

He said he knew that his duty was to love God in all things, and he worked as hard as he could to do this. So he had no need of anyone to guide him. He had much need, however, of someone to hear his confession and absolve him. He was very aware of his faults, but did not let them get him down – he confessed them to God without trying to make excuses. Once he had done that, he returned quietly to his usual practice of love and worship.

When he had been troubled he had not spoken to anybody. He had believed that God was with him, and so it had been enough to live for Him, doing everything with a desire to please God by it, whatever might come of it.

Idle thoughts spoil everything. Evil begins there. We ought to put away every thought that is not relevant to our immediate business, or to our final salvation, and then return to our conversation with God.

To begin with, he had spent the whole of the time of prayer in putting away thoughts and then falling back into them. He never could pray according to a rule as some do. At first he had meditated for a little while, but that had gone in a way he could not explain.

✠

He said that all penance and other disciplines are useless unless they lead to union with God by love. He had thought hard about this, and decided that the best way was to go straight to God by a constant love, and by doing all things out of love for God.

We have to understand the different between knowing and desiring. Knowing rightly does not matter very much; desiring rightly is everything. The only thing we should care about is loving and enjoying God.

Nothing we can do can achieve anything apart from love. We cannot erase a single sin. We should expect confidently that our sins will be forgiven through the blood of Jesus Christ, and strive only to love Him with all our hearts. God seems to give the best things to the greatest sinners, more so than those who remain relatively innocent. This highlights God's mercy.

Brother Lawrence never thought of death, or of his sins, or of heaven, or of hell. He thought only of doing little things out of love for God – little things, because he could not do great things. He realized that he could please God in anything and everything.

The worst physical pain was nothing compared to the internal trouble he had faced, and the greatest pleasures in the world are nothing compared to spiritual joys. Knowing this, Brother Lawrence cared for nothing and feared nothing – asking nothing of God but that he would not offend Him.

He never worried about anything. 'When I realize that I have failed,' he says, 'I admit it cheerfully and say that this is normal for me, I would never do anything else left to myself. If I succeed, I give thanks to God, and acknowledge that it all comes from Him.'

More to think and pray ...

1. Be encouraged! It is impossible to do anything for God and not receive his blessing and reward. Reflect on the time when your efforts or service seem to have been less than fruitful and remember that God has used them in his own way and will return them to you with his favour.

2. What does it mean for you to 'desire' and 'enjoy' God? How might you desire and enjoy him more?

3. 'He hadn't a worry in the world.' Imagine what life would be without worry. Brother Lawrence suggests that this is how Jesus would have his followers live. Take time to offer you worries in the form of prayers and walk away from them knowing that the worries themselves are not part of God's plan for your life.

Dorothy L. Sayers

'Before ascending the Mountain, Dante's face must be cleansed from the tears he shed in Hell. The penitent's first duty is cheerfulness: having recognised his sin he must put it out of his mind and not wallow in self-pity and self-reproach, which are forms of egotism.'

Commentary on Dante's Purgatorio

Chapter Twenty-three

Happy Correction

THIS POEM, BY MARIANNE FARNINGHAM, IS CALLED 'DISCIPLINE' AND WAS INSPIRED BY THE WORDS OF JOB 5:17: 'HAPPY IS THE MAN WHO GOD CORRECTS.'

Discipline

'He chastens whom He loves.' Even in childhood
    We pondered o'er the words with pensive thought;
In the green meadows and the flower-filled wild wood
    This lesson grave was into being wrought;
But 'twas a mystery for later years
To know that Love itself could cause our tears.

Yet is it so; and often as we ponder
    Over the love of God made manifest,
Thinking of troubles He has blessed, we wonder,
    Yet know that these have brought us of life's best;
Sorrow and pain have kept us at His side,
Else had we fallen low and wandered wide.

We have not walked alone. Ever the Father
    Has given His Son to love and comfort us:
Not all in vain our sorrow, but the rather
    We thank Him that He has corrected thus
Those who had sinned, and burnt away with fire
Unworthy things, and cleansed the heart's desire.

Therefore be brave again, O sister, brother,
    Accept the touch, the hurts, the hand that stays,
For God corrects in love, because no other
    Could so uplift us into higher ways;

To give us wealth of soul, to conquer sin,
God keeps His children under discipline.

The after fruits of sorrow are our gain,
　　The lessons of our youth enrich our age,
Gladness and peace come to us after pain,
　　And God's corrections are our heritage;
Be not afraid to walk with God in light,
For sometimes sweetest songs are sung at night.

More to think and pray ...

1. Go through the poem again and pick out the lines that resonate most strongly with you.
2. Ask why these particular words and phrases stand out and take time to identify the memories and experiences that they strike a chord against.
3. Thank God for these times, his presence with you and the lessons learned.

Chapter Twenty-four

Daily Grind?

THIS EXTRACT IS TAKEN FROM THE
RULE OF ST BENEDICT.

It is dangerous to be unoccupied. Monks should therefore have set times for work, as well as set times for prayer and reading.

We suggest that times for both might be arranged like this: between Easter and the beginning of October, they can spend mornings from after morning prayer until about 10 a.m. doing whatever work needs to be done. Then, until noon, they should read. After lunch, they may rest in silence – if one brother wants to read privately, he may, so long as he does not disturb the others. The 3 o'clock prayers can be said a little early, an hour or so, and then they can return to work until evening prayers around 5 p.m. If local conditions or the poverty of the community forces them to harvest their own crops, they shouldn't worry – when they live by the labour of their own hands, like our fathers and the apostles did, then they are truly monks. But do everything gently to protect the weak.

From the beginning of October to the start of Lent, the brothers ought to give themselves to reading until about 9 a.m. Then they can say the mid-morning prayers, and work until the 3 o'clock prayers. Then, after a meal, they will give themselves to reading, or to the psalms.

Through Lent they should be free to read until about 9.30 a.m., then they will work until 3 p.m. During Lent, each brother will be given a book from the library, and should read it straight through. These books should be given out at the beginning of Lent.

Above all, one or two elders of the community should be set aside to roam the monastery while the brothers are reading. They are to make sure that no brother is lazy enough to waste time, or gossip, and so neglect reading – not only harming himself, but distracting others! If, unhappily, someone is discovered like this, he should be warned twice. If he does not change, he should suffer the set punishments as a warning to others. Brothers should not mix together at inappropriate times.

On Sundays, everyone should read, except those who have particular duties. If anyone is so careless and lazy that he cannot or will not study and read, give him some work, so he won't be idle.

Brothers who are ill or weak should be given work, or a craft, that will keep them busy without destroying them or driving them away. The abbot must think about their weaknesses.

More to think and pray ...

1. Benedict suggests a pattern of work, public prayer, and private prayer and study that varies according to the seasons; what sort of patterns might work in your life?
2. In summer, Benedict advises all monks to rest in the heat of the day (he lived in Italy); are there times you should rest more?
3. Reading is at the heart of Benedict's rule. Would reading more help you?

Prince Metternich (1773–1859)

'The word "freedom" means for me not a point of departure but a genuine point of arrival. The point of departure is defined by the word "order". Freedom cannot exist without the concept of order.'

Mein Politisches Testament in
Aus Metternich's Nachgelassnen Papieren
(ed. A. von Klinkowstöm, 1880) vol. 8, p. 233

Chapter Twenty-five

Ways to Pray

THIS EXTRACT IS TAKEN FROM *THE WAY OF PERFECTION*
BY TERESA OF AVILA.

Daughters, don't be discouraged by how much there is to think about before you start this holy journey. It is the royal road to heaven! It leads to such precious treasures – of course it seems a difficult way! But we will get to a point when we see that everything it has cost us has still been nothing at all, compared to the great prize we have gained.

What of those who want to walk this way and will not stop until they reach their journey's end, the place where they can drink the water of life itself? (I've read that this is the right way to begin in a book, or actually several books, but it is worth me making the point again.) It is important – it is absolutely vital – that we begin by making a serious and determined commitment not to stop until we reach the end. Whatever turns up, whatever happens, however hard we have to work, whether we get to the end or die still on the road or cannot face the difficulties that we meet – even if the whole world should fall apart around us – we must be determined to keep going. People keep telling us 'it's dangerous!' 'John was lost doing this!'; 'Moira went completely wrong!'; 'Franklin, who was always praying, still fell into sin!'; 'This is bad for virtue!'; 'Women should not do this; they will become deluded!'; 'They should stick to housework!'; 'Women have no use for serious spiritual matters!'; 'They don't need to do anything more than say the Lord's Prayer and the Hail Mary!'. (This last comment is quite right, of course, sisters. It is always good to base your prayer on prayers that the Lord Himself prayed. People are quite right to say this and there should be no need for other systems of prayer, or for any books at all – only, we are weak and lukewarm.)

I am speaking to people who struggle to come home by meditating on other mysteries. They think they need special methods of prayer; some of them have such ingenious minds that nothing is ever good enough for them. So I intend to lay down some rules for our prayer – for the beginning, the middle, and the end. I won't spend too long on the higher levels – no-one can take your books from you, and if you are studious and humble, you need nothing more.

I have always loved the words of the Gospels. I have benefited more from them than from the most carefully organized books – especially books whose authors were of questionable orthodoxy, which I have never wanted to read. I will keep close to this master of wisdom, and He may perhaps give you some pointers that will help you. I am not going to try to explain these divine prayers: I would not presume to do that, and there are many published explanations already (even if there were none, I could not do it). I will write down a few thoughts about the Lord's Prayer. Sometimes, even when we are most anxious to feed our devotion, reading many books will kill it. When a good teacher is giving a lesson, he treats the pupil kindly. He tries to make the lesson fun, and does everything to promote learning. So our divine Teacher will do for us.

More to think and pray …

1. Teresa is concerned to warn her nuns against people who tell them that it is dangerous to walk the way of discipleship; what warnings or discouragements do you face from people around you?
2. In what ways might God want to make your learning about prayer 'fun'?
3. How could you focus more on the Lord's prayer, and the words of the gospels, in your prayers?

Chapter Twenty-six

Hospitality and Judgement

THIS EXTRACT WAS TAKEN FROM THE WRITINGS OF
THE DESERT FATHERS.

Some brothers left a monastery to go into the desert, and they came
to a hermit. He received them cheerfully. He saw how tired they
were, so prepared a meal before the usual time, and brought out
everything he had to refresh them (such hospitality is normal among
the desert hermits). When evening came, they recited the twelve
psalms set, and they did the same at night. Later, he was praying
quietly alone, and he heard them saying to each other 'They live
more easily here in the desert than we do in the monastery!'

Early the next morning, they got ready to leave to visit the
neighbouring Father. Their host said to them, 'Give him my
greetings, and say to him, "Do not water the vegetables".' They
did this. When he heard them, the other Father understood what
was meant, and he kept the brothers at work until evening.
When evening came, he recited the whole of the great liturgy and
then said 'We should stop now because you are tired.' Then he
added 'We do not eat every day, but for your sakes we will have
something.' He brought out dry bread and salt, saying 'For your
sakes, we will feast!' then he poured a little vinegar on the salt.
When they had finished eating, they said the liturgy until the sun
was nearly up. Then he said to them, 'We can't keep my whole
rule of life – for your sakes, you must take a little rest, for you
are strangers.' When morning came, they wanted to run away,
but he prevented them, saying 'Stay here for a while – at least
three days according to the commandment – that is the desert
way. When they saw that he would not send them away, they
rose and escaped secretly.

A brother asked one of the Fathers 'If I happen to fall asleep and miss the right time for saying prayers, I no longer want to pray, because I am afraid of what people will think.' The Father said to him, 'If you sleep till morning, get up, shut the door and windows, and say the prayers. Scripture says, after all, "The day is yours, and the night also" [Ps. 73:16]. Truly, God is glorified at every hour of the day!'

✠

Some monks travelled from Egypt to Scetis to visit the Fathers. The Fathers were hungry because of their discipline, and they ate greedily. This shocked the monks. When the priest discovered this, he wanted to teach them a lesson, so he told the people in church, 'My brothers, increase your discipline – fast!' When the Egyptian visitors wanted to leave, he would not let them.

After the first day of fasting, the visitors were becoming ill. The priest made them fast every other day, whereas the monks of Scetis fasted all week. Come Saturday, the Egyptians and the Fathers sat down to eat together. The Egyptians fell on the food greedily, so one of the Fathers took them aside and said, 'Eat sensibly, like monks!' One of them pushed him away, however, saying 'Leave me alone! I am starving! I've had nothing cooked all week!' The Father said to him 'You've eaten every other day – if you're so exhausted after that, how can you be shocked by brothers who always follow a discipline like this?' Then the Egyptians asked the monks of Scetis to forgive them and left cheerfully because of what they had learnt.

✠

A brother asked one of the Fathers if it was sinful to have evil thoughts. There was a discussion on the subject. Some said 'Yes, it defiles you.' Others said 'No – just look at us! If this were so, we could not be saved! What matters is not the thoughts, but making sure we do not carry them out.'

The brother went to a very experienced Father to ask him about this. He said, 'Each one is asked to live according to his capacity.' The brother begged the Father, 'For the Lord's sake, please explain this saying!' The Father said to him, 'Suppose something very tempting was put here, and two brothers came in, one much further along the way than the other. The one whose perfection is advanced will think 'I would like to have that thing!' but he does not let the thought last – he cuts it off as soon as it forms, and he is not stained by it. But the one who is not so far along desires the thing, and his thought stays with it – but if he doesn't take it, he also is not defiled.'

More to think and pray ...

1. The first and third stories represent a common theme in the desert sayings, the danger of judging another harshly because you do not know their circumstances. Have you ever been the victim of this? How could you avoid doing it to other people in future?

2. Would you be prepared to leave your habits of prayer to be hospitable to ungrateful guests? Should you?

3. Do you agree with the analysis of the Father in the last story? Why, or why not?

Chapter Twenty-seven

What Disciples Know

THIS EXTRACT IS FROM A SERMON BY JOHN BUNYAN ENTITLED 'THE SAINT'S KNOWLEDGE OF CHRIST, OR THE UNSEARCHABLE RICHES OF CHRIST'.

Jesus loves us more than we'll ever know. But how useful is it for us to know that? Surely, it would be more helpful if we could fully understand just how much he does love us.

However it turns out that there is a real advantage in us knowing the size and scope of God's love even though it is beyond both our measure and comprehension. A New Testament writer once prayed that we, 'being rooted and grounded in love, may be able to comprehend with all the saints … the width the length and depth and height' of God's love and so 'know the love of Christ which passes knowledge,' so that we might 'be filled with all the fullness of God' [Eph. 3:17–20, NKJV].

By knowing the height, depth and breadth of Christ's love, I know just how much he has in reserve should I lose everything else. On the day that I hit rock bottom, I am content to stand on the rock; my feet being planted on the firmest love. And if Jesus' love is beyond understanding then I can be sure of it in times when I simply don't understand what's going on. Whether it's temptation's turmoil, sin's sadness or the depths of despair, when I can no longer grasp why or how anyone can love me, I know that God does for Christ's love surpasses understanding.

In addition, when Satan dissuades me from talking to my Father and taunts me with my own ineloquence, my answer is ready and waiting for him: 'God loves me beyond understanding.' If he sends trials and troubles, while I may not understand how, I know that Christ will carry me through … In my worst nightmare,

when confronted with doubt and the fearful possibility that God's grace is either insufficient or non-existent the answer is at hand for God's love is beyond my understanding....
To know this seemingly unfathomable truth is to experience the liberty of Christianity.... If disciples fail to grasp it they will walk as if they were in manacles and serve as though they wearing handcuffs. But with this truth under their belts their steps will straighten and extend and they will walk freer and taller than ever before.
The story is told of two men. Having heard warnings of an impending drought, the first had stored gallons of water around his house. The second did likewise and then discovered a natural spring at the bottom of his garden. When a drought came their way it was the latter who continued to live in freedom and liberty despite the difficulty. In the same way, if one disciple rests content to know all there is to know of Jesus but does not contemplate what is unknowable and a second commits himself to both forms of knowledge, which one is most likely to live as a prince? Which one is most likely to live in godly largeness of heart and freedom of imagination? Which will have the most to live and love for? Which will be most ready to face the trials and temptations that come their way? Well, the latter of course.
Having experienced the all-surpassing love of Jesus, the disciple journeys on with increased hope and eagerness for all that God has placed before him [Phil. 3:12–21]. The kind of slovenly and carnal content that all too often passes for Christianity is caused solely by an ignorance of God's limitless love. Thinking that they know it all stops many from seeking after more. Yet the imperfections of our own minds and the eternal nature of Christ's love mean that there is infinitely more of him left to know and experience....
But this is not all. There is a knowledge of God's love that we cannot possess until we are possessed by heaven.... One day we will be swallowed whole in this unknowable and unending love....
Knowing the love that surpasses understanding is a thoroughly fruitful experience. While some forms of knowledge are empty and lonely, the knowledge of God's love overflows with blessing. It fills our own small souls with the entire fullness of God.

God is in Christ, and makes himself known to us by the love of Christ. As John writes, those who do 'not abide in Christ, do not have God' in their lives. But those who abide in Christ have 'both the Father and the Son' [2 Jn. 1:9]. It follows, then, that those who have the smallest knowledge of Christ have God in their lives. Furthermore, those who have the largest knowledge are all the more full of him....

What can be said of those disciples who are full of God? These followers sweeten their churches, bring glory to God and authenticate our faith. It is the knowledge of our God and his love – the love that surpasses understanding – that can make us into these kinds of disciples.

More to pray and think ...

1. How has God revealed himself to you in new ways over these past weeks? Ask him to reveal himself more in weeks to come.
2. Thank God for the infinite riches already yours in Jesus. Remember, if you lose everything, what you have in him will be enough.
3. How have you sweetened the life of your church congregation, fellow believers and local community of late?

John Newton (1725–1807)

'How sweet the name of Jesus sounds in a believer's ear! It soothes his sorrows, heals his wounds, and drives away his fear.'

Olney Hymns (1779),
'How Sweet the Name of Jesus Sounds'

Chapter Twenty-eight

Turn, Turn, Turn

THIS IS AN EXTRACT FROM A SERMON ENTITLED
'REPENT AND BELIEVE', PREACHED IN LONDONDERRY
IN 1767 BY JOHN WESLEY, FROM MARK 1:15.

We generally think that repentance marks the beginning of our life with Christ; as though it is the front door of faith that we must first open before beginning our journey with Jesus. ... And while this is undoubtedly true, this first special act of repentance is by no means our last. In another sense of the word, 'repentance', that decision we make to turn towards Christ, becomes habitual. In short, if we truly believe in the gospel, and wish to advance our faith, we must keep on turning towards God's kingdom. However, if we have already been forgiven and justified by Christ, how and why should we continue to repent?

Repentance usually describes that inner change of direction whereby we turn from sin to holiness. But having already made this call, the believer pursues repentance in a different way. It starts with a rigorous reality check. It is born out of our brokenness. For as we know we are forever children of God we also remain painfully aware of our guilt and fallibility.

In the first burst of Christian faith it is natural to feel that our sins have been buried, dug over and destroyed. Momentarily, there is no darkness in our hearts and we can hardly imagine it creeping back in. But soon we arrive at the mature acknowledgement that while sin may not reign over us it certainly remains in us. It is this continuing conviction that leads to the kind of repentance we are talking about. ...

What's more, without this ongoing repentance our walk with Christ will stall or stop. Put another way, until we understand the nature of our disease it is impossible to prescribe a lasting cure. The act of turning to Christ in all of our todays enables us to hear and believe the great news he has for us.

This act of repentance is different from the act of justification. In accepting the good news of God's story of salvation we can rejoice knowing that our eternal status is the same as that of the risen Jesus. To be justified is to know that our eternal destiny is not dependent on our achievements (or lack of them, for that matter). Because of Christ, it is just as if I hadn't sinned. However, the one who saves us from sin and death, once and for all, is also able to save us from the effects of sin and death in the here and now. He can save us from our present faults and failings, from misdemeanours both meant and unmeant, from the things that cling to us and the hurts that harm us. While this may appear unlikely or unrealistic, implausible or impossible, God would remind us that, in Christ, all things are possible. Furthermore, over and over, he has promised us his power in this regard (Deut. 30:6; Ezek. 36:25; Lk. 1:68). . . .

As we daily turn to Jesus, we have great reason to rejoice and believe that he is willing and able to purify every part of us, to deep clean our lives by the power of his Spirit. This is what we long for. The renewing work of our Creator, the healing touch of a Great Physician and the intimate embrace of the Lover of our Soul. Only in turning to him can we ever be completely and continually clean. But can he do this today or must we wait for tomorrow or perhaps the day after? Let's allow God's word do the talking: 'Today, please listen, don't turn a deaf ear ... The promise of "arrival" and "rest" is still there for God's people ... And at the end of the journey we'll surely rest with God. So let's keep at it and eventually arrive at the place of rest, not drop out through some sort of disobedience' [Heb. 4:6–8, *The Message*]. . . .

Some might conclude then that when God justified us he also sanctified us; that in taking away our sin he made us wholly holy and in forgiving our fallenness he exorcised all our sin. As we mentioned before, while it is true that Jesus' death delivered us from the dominion of death and sin, we can by no means claim to be sin-free. In our heart of hearts we are all too familiar with our worldly ways, our pride and selfishness, angers and lusts. Denying these realities requires dangerous delusion. And yet the perpetuity of our faults and failings can undermine our hope for freedom, be it in a gradual process or momentary miracle.

Knowledge of God's utter acceptance of us and the assurance of our salvation are essential items for the Christian disciple as we follow Christ. That said, the pilgrim must not forget the old baggage, which they regrettably continue to carry along the way. Rather our deepest convictions should prompt us to turn once again to our travelling companion in search of the act of forgiveness, healing and transformation that only he can assist in....

In conclusion, let's not forget that Christ is not only our companion but our Priest and our King. He is able to walk with us, qualified to represent us before God and able to effect his beneficent rule over every aspect of our lives, whether we believe it or not. Whenever we pledge ourselves as members of his kingdom and loyal subjects of his rule, his purity of power rains down on us and his all-conquering grace abolishes our darkness. In these moments of repentance, when we turn to him again, our every thought and feeling, word and work becomes a new act of obedience to Christ.

More to think and pray ...

1. While Jesus certainly doesn't ask that his disciples live in perpetual guilt he does encourage us to turn to him over and over again. How might we make repentance a more regular and positive part of our life with him?

2. Meditate on Ezekiel 36:24–38. Read this passage and rejoice in the promise that God makes to his people both now and then.

3. Take time to thank God for the freedom and forgiveness that are ours in him. Reflect on how we can enjoy this sin-free state to the utmost. In what ways do we swap his righteousness for our dirty rags?

Chapter Twenty-nine

Three Things on Prayer

THIS EXTRACT IS TAKEN FROM *REVELATIONS OF DIVINE LOVE*, BY MOTHER JULIAN OF NORWICH.

Our Lord God wants us to understand rightly three things concerning prayer. The first is from whom and how our praying begins – He shows who it comes from when He says 'I am the foundation'; and He shows how, by His goodness, when He says 'First is my will.' The second thing is how we should normally pray – our will should be joyfully transformed into the will of our Lord; this is what He means when He says 'I make you desire it.' As for the third, He wants us to know the proper fruit, the aim, of our prayers, which is to be one with our Lord, like Him in every way. The whole of this precious vision was revealed for this purpose. He will help us, and we shall make His promises come to reality. May He be blessed!

This is God's will: that our prayers and our trust should both spread wide. If we do not trust as much as we pray, we do not truly honour God in our prayers, and we hinder and pain ourselves. I think that the cause is this: we do not realize that our prayers arise from the Lord, who is the foundation of them all, and nor do we know that our prayer is given to us by the grace of His love. If we knew this, we would be sure that God would give us everything we desire. No-one really asks for grace and mercy without first being given both grace and mercy. Sometimes we feel that we have prayed for a long time, and yet not (we think) received what we asked for. We should not be sad about this; I am sure that in the Lord's purpose we need only wait for a better time, or for more grace, or for a better gift …

God's gracious light wants to show us these things: first, our noble and excellent creation; second our costly and precious renewal; third, everything He has made beneath is for our use, which He upholds out of love for us. This is what He means, then, as if He actually said to us, 'Look! See, I have done all of this before you even prayed! Now you exist, and now you can pray to me.' We should know that God has done the greatest things that we needed, as the Church teaches. We should think about this, and be thankful, and pray for the thing that now needs doing. What now needs doing? He should rule over us, and guide us to worship Him in this life, and bring us to His eternal joys. He has already done everything necessary for this.

This is what He means: we must see that He is doing this and so we must pray for it. We need both of these; if we pray without seeing what God is doing, we become sad and we start doubting, which does not glorify God. If we see what God is doing, but don't pray, we are not doing what we should, and that must not happen. If we see what God is doing and pray for it, God is glorified and we benefit. God desires that we should pray for everything He has determined to do, particularly or in general. This is joy and delight to God, and we shall gain thanks and honour from it, beyond anything we can understand. Prayer is a true knowledge of the fullness of joy which is to come, a sure trust that it will come, and a great longing for it. We long because we lack the delight which God intended us for, and we trust because we understand and love what out Saviour has done for us. Our Lord watches us continually as we perform these two actions. They are our duty, and His goodness will not let Him ask of us anything less. We must try as hard as we can; when we are done, we will still think it is nothing – because, indeed, it is. If we do the best we can, however, and ask honestly for mercy and for grace, we will find everything we need in Him. This is what he means when He says 'I am the foundation of your prayers'. So in this delightful word, I saw how all our weaknesses and all our doubts and fears are overcome.

More to think and pray ...

1. The reason that Christians say, 'Our Father' is because we never pray alone. We are joined in our prayers by all of God's people, the fellowship of the saints and Jesus himself. Remembering this, pray the prayer that Jesus taught to his disciples and know that he joins us and intercedes on our behalf.
2. Your Kingdom come, your will be done. Take time to ask God to bend and blend your will with his. Pray that through your conversation with him that you might further resemble Jesus.
3. Take time to identify things that God is doing in and around your life and community. Thank him for these and ask him to pinpoint more miracles in days to come.

Contemplation

Contemplation, or 'contemplative prayer' is a common term in Christian spiritual writing. It refers to a special gift of God, when God allows the praying heart to 'see' or contemplate Him directly. This meeting with God in prayer is sometimes described as the goal of all prayer.

Chapter Thirty

The Pearl Beyond Price

THESE POEMS ARE TAKEN FROM *THE TEMPLE*,
BY GEORGE HERBERT.

The Pearl (Mt. 13)

I Know the ways of Learning; both the head
And pipes that feed the press, and make it run;
What reason hath from nature borrowed,
Or of its self, like a good housewife, spun
In laws and policy; what the stars conspire,
What willing nature speaks, what forced by fire;
Both the old discoveries, and the new-found seas,[1]
The stock and surplus, cause and history:
All these stand open, or I have the keys:
     Yet I love thee.

I know the ways of Honour, what maintains
The quick returns of courtesy and wit:
In vies of favours whether party gains,
When glory swells the heart, and moldeth it
To all expressions both of hand and eye,
Which on the world a true-love-knot may tie,
And bear the bundle, wheresoever it goes:
How many drams of spirit there must be
To sell my life unto my friends or foes:
     Yet I love thee.

---

[1] Herbert is writing in the age of discovery, when European sailors were sailing to parts of the world they had never known about before.

I know the ways of Pleasure, the sweet strains,
The lullings and the relishes of it;
The propositions of hot blood and brains;
What mirth and music mean; what love and wit
Have done these twenty hundred years, and more:
I know the projects of unbridled store:
My stuff is flesh, not brass; my senses live,
And grumble oft, that they have more in me
Then he that curbs them, being but one to five:
                    Yet I love thee.

I know all these, and have them in my hand:
Therefore not sealed, but with open eyes
I fly to thee, and fully understand
Both the main sale, and the commodities;
And at what rate and price I have thy love;
With all the circumstances that may move:
Yet through these labyrinths, not my grovelling wit,
But thy silk twist let down from heaven to me,
Did both conduct and teach me, how by it
                    To climb to thee.

Obedience

My God, if writings may
Convey a Lordship any way
Whither the buyer and the seller please;
Let it not thee displease,
If this poor paper do as much as they.

On it my heart doth bleed
As many lines, as there doth need
To pass itself and all it hath to thee.
To which I do agree,
And here present it as my special deed.

If that hereafter Pleasure
Cavil, and claim her part and measure,
As if this passed with a reservation,
Or some such words in fashion;
I here exclude the wrangler from thy treasure.

O let thy sacred will
All thy delight in me fulfil!
Let me not think an action mine own way,
But as thy love shall sway,
Resigning up the rudder to thy skill.

Lord, what is man to thee,
That thou shouldst mind a rotten tree?
Yet since thou canst not choose but see my actions;
So great are thy perfections,
Thou mayst as well my actions guide, as see.

Besides, thy death and blood
Showed a strange love to all our good:
Thy sorrows were in earnest; no faint proffer,
Or superficial offer
Of what we might not take, or be withstood.

Wherefore I all forgo:
To one word only I say, No:
Where in the deed there was an intimation
Of a gift or donation,
Lord, let it now by way of purchase go.

He that will pass his land,
As I have mine, may set his hand
And heart unto this deed, when he hath read;
And make the purchase spread
To both our goods, if he to it will stand.

How happy were my part,
If some kind man would thrust his heart
Into these lines; till in heaven's court of rolls
They were by winged souls
Entered for both, far above their desert!

More to think and pray ...

1. The first poem suggests that learning, honour and pleasure can all get in the way of loving God. Does this ring true in your experience? In what ways? What can you do to prevent the problem?

2. Many of the writers in this book suggest the need for a moment of serious surrender to God, and Herbert offers an example in the first stanzas of the second poem. Is this something you can imagine doing?

SECTION FOUR

✠

WORKING

Chapter Thirty-one

The World as Hazelnut

THIS EXTRACT IS TAKEN FROM *REVELATIONS OF DIVINE LOVE*, BY MOTHER JULIAN OF NORWICH.

At the same time the Lord gave me a vision of how intimately He loves us. I saw that He is everything that is good and helpful for us. He clothes us in Himself, wrapping us around with His love, embracing and surrounding us with tender love. He can never leave us, because He is everything that is good to us, as I understand it.

In the vision He showed me a little thing, about the size of a hazelnut in the palm of my hand. It was round, like a ball. I gazed at it in my imagination and thought 'What is that?' And the answer came to me: 'This is the whole creation!' I was amazed that it continued to exist, because it seemed so small and fragile. An answer came to my mind again: 'It continues, and always will, because God loves it – everything that exists, exists by the love of God.'

I saw three truths about this tiny thing: first, God made it; second, God loves it; third, God holds it close. But what the Creator, the Lover, the Maker is to me, I do not know – until I become one with Him, I can never know true peace or real happiness. No, not until I am so joined to Him that there is nothing at all created between my God and me.

We need to know how tiny created things are – all of them, even the biggest. Then we can put aside everything created, and love and hold God the Creator. This is why our hearts are uneasy: we look for satisfaction here, where everything is so trivial, where there is no rest to be found. Instead, we should look to God, all-powerful, all-wise, all-good. He is rest itself. God wants us to know Him. He delights when we find rest in Him. He knows that nothing other than Him can bring us true satisfaction, and this is why our hearts cannot be at rest until we put aside everything but God. When we deliberately put everything aside for love, aiming to have Him who is everything, then we can find true peace.

Our Lord God also showed me that He delights when a simple heart comes to Him, without hiding anything, honestly, and even presuming on His friendship. As I understand my vision, this is the normal desire of the heart that the Holy Spirit has entered; such a heart will say 'God, out of your goodness, give me – yourself. Only you are enough for me; if I asked anything less of you, I would not honour you properly. And if I asked anything less, I would be left needing more – only in you can I have everything.' Words like these come from the heart, and grasp hold of God's own desire, and God's goodness. God's goodness includes all His creatures, and everything He has done. God's goodness is far, far more than anything we might ask or even imagine. It is endless and fathomless, just as God Himself is endless and fathomless. He made us for Himself alone, and renewed us by His suffering on the cross, and cares for us in His wonderful love. This is the demonstration of His goodness....

I am no good, even though I received this vision, unless it leads me to love God better. If you, reading it, love God better, the vision is for you, not for me. I don't say this to the wise, who know it already, but I say it to anyone who does not yet understand. Let this support and comfort you – we all need comfort. I was certainly not shown that God loved me any better than the least of His people – I'm sure, indeed, that there are many people who never had a vision, but just the normal teachings of the church, and who love God better than I do. I am nothing, considering just me myself; but I hope that I am one in love with my fellow Christians. Salvation and life depend on being at one with God's people. God is all that is good; God has created all that is created, and God loves every creature. So whoever loves other Christians – all of them! – for God's sake loves all that is. Because in those who will be saved is included everything – I mean, everything created, and the Creator of everything. God dwells in the human heart, and so the human being is all. I hope that, by God's grace, anyone who thinks about this will be taught truth and comforted greatly (if comfort is needed). I am talking about people who will be saved, because at this time God showed me no others.

More to think and pray ...

1. We have thought often about what it means to know that God is with us, alongside us on the road, in the person of Jesus. In this passage Julian presses us to know that God also dwells in us and that we live in him. Take some time to ponder this awesome, life-changing mystery.

2. Julian reminds us that love is not limited to individuals or one particular race or species. The love that God has for us is the love he has for the whole creation. How should the knowledge that God loves the whole world impact the way we think about faith and life? How does this impact our views on the environment, politics, poverty and social justice, etc.?

Percy Dearmer (1867–1936)

English clergyman

'Jesu, good above all other,
Gentle Child of gentle Mother,
In a stable born our Brother,
Give us grace to persevere.'

'Jesu, good above all other'
(1906 hymn)

Chapter Thirty-two

The Kingdom Within

THIS EXTRACT IS TAKEN FROM THE *IMITATION OF CHRIST* BY THOMAS À KEMPIS.

1. 'The Kingdom of God is within you,' says the Lord [Lk. 17:21]. So turn your whole heart to God, abandon this miserable world, and your soul will find peace. Learn to despise whatever is without, and to give yourself to what is within, and you will see the Kingdom of God come in you. For the Kingdom of God is peace and joy in the Holy Spirit, which is not given to the ungodly. Christ will come to you, displaying his goodness, if you have prepared a dwelling-place for Him. All His glory and beauty are inward, and he pleases to live within. He often comes to the heart, bringing sweet conversation, gracious help, much peace and astonishing fellowship.

2. So come, faithful heart, prepare yourself for this Bridegroom, so that He will be prepared to come to you and to live in you. For He says, 'If anyone loves me, they will keep my word, and we will come to them, and make our dwelling with them' [Jn. 14:15–21]. Give Christ a place, then, and refuse entry to all others. When you have Christ, you are rich, and have enough of everything! He will provide for you, and will watch out for you in everything, so there is no need to put your hope in other human beings. For humans change rapidly and disappear; Christ remains for eternity, and stands firm until the end.

3. Do not place your confidence in humanity, weak and mortal, even if a particular person is both useful to you and cherished. Nor should we be too sorrowful if someone stands or speaks against us. Someone who is on your side today can turn

against you tomorrow, and often change like the wind. Put
your confidence in God! Let Him be your fear, and your love!
He will answer for you, and will give blessings as is best. You
do not have any 'continuing city' here; wherever you are, you
are a stranger and a pilgrim. You will find no rest, until you
are united with Christ within.

4. Why look around here? This is not your resting place! Your
home must be in heaven, and earthly things are merely sights
you pass by on the way there. Everything passes, and you will
also. Make sure that you do not become too involved, unless
you are caught, and die! Fix your mind on the Most High,
and pray without ceasing to Christ. If you do not know how
to discover high and heavenly things, rest in the sufferings of
Christ, and willingly focus on His sacred wounds. For if you
devoutly flee to the wounds and precious scars of Jesus, you
will feel great comfort in troubles, and you will not care much
for the hard words said against you.

5. Christ was despised by human beings on earth, and in His
greatest need He was insulted and abandoned by those who
knew Him, by His friends. What makes you think you can
complain about anyone? Christ had his enemies and slanderers;
do you think you should have nothing but friends and
supporters? You cannot win a reward for patience if you have
not borne any trouble! If you do not want to face opposition,
how can you be Christ's friend? Endure with Christ, endure
for Christ, if you wish to reign with Christ!

6. If you have just once entered into the heart of Jesus, and tasted
a little of His burning love, then you will care nothing for your
own comfort or inconvenience, but will instead rejoice at the
hatred shown you. The love of Jesus teaches us our own true
value, after all! Someone who loves Jesus and the truth, whose
heart is true, who is free from inappropriate affections – this
person can freely turn to God, and rise up and rest.

7. If you can value things for what they are worth, and not what
people tell you they are worth, you are wise, and have learnt
more from God than from other people. If you know how
to walk the way of your heart, not caring too much about
external things, you will not wait for particular places and

times, or special devotional practices. Someone like this can bring themselves home to themselves, because they are never given too much to external things. If you have to work, it will not get in your way; you will be able to adapt to things that happen. If your life is together within and without, you will not worry much about the strange things other people do. We only become hindered and distracted as we let things affect us from without.

8. If everything was right with you, if you were properly cleansed, everything would work together for your good and profit. This is why so many things upset and disturb you, you know – you are not yet truly dead to yourself, separated from all mundane things. Nothing stains and ties down the human heart so much as an improper love for created things. If you give up looking for pleasure and help without, you will see divine things, and be able to rejoice within.

More to think and pray ...

1. How might we better see our world through God's eyes? What aspects and issues in your day-to-day existence concern him most?

2. What does it mean to live life with an eternal perspective? Take time to consider the things in your life that have a more eternal significance.

3. Take time to pray and ask God to provide his perspective on your life and community.

Chapter Thirty-three

Being Born Again

THESE EXTRACTS ARE TAKEN FROM A SERMON BY
JOHN BUNYAN ON JOHN 1:13. THIS MESSAGE WAS THE
LAST HE EVER GAVE.

So what are the consequences of being born again?
Upon entering the world, the first thing a baby does is to
scream and cry. A silent newborn is a cause to worry or reason
to mourn. Similarly, if we claim to be children of God but are
unprepared to make a noise about our new-found faith, then
we have no spiritual life. If you are born again you are a 'crier',
a heaven-crier who shouts to God, 'Please, save me!' Yet, how
many prayerless preachers are there in the church and how many
jobbing theologians hardly ever pray? While there may be places,
people and policies that prohibit prayer, this truth remains: if we
are born again we must pray.

The newborn child not only makes a noise but craves its
mother's breast. Hence, Peter notes that God's children are
dependent on the nourishing milk of God's Word. If we are born
again we will be hungry for God; we will live off the promises in
his Word [1 Pet. 2:2–3].

Secondly, it is not only natural for a child to cry, but it must
crave the breast, it cannot live without the breast; therefore
Peter makes this the true test of a newborn believer. Born again
Christians grow as they drink the milk of God's Word. Do we
have that hunger and thirst for God's Word? For those who are
yet to be born again this hunger and thirst are meaningless. To
someone who doesn't know Christ, the promise of Christ is
meaningless; they have no appetite for it. They are content to
eat junk food, happy to be unhealthy. Some would even choose a

whorehouse over heaven. However, those of us who live in Christ find newness of life. All the empty appetites we once thought promising have been replaced by a deep hunger for the eternal promises in God's Word.

Thirdly, a newborn child, having left the womb, requires warmth if it is to survive. In the same way that his mother wrapped Jesus in sheets and blankets, so those who are born again need the warm embrace of Christ. Those away from Christ find other fires upon which to warm themselves but disciples look to Jesus. What's more, in the same way as a mother dresses her child in the finest clothes in order to show off her 'pride and joy', so too God promises to bejewel his children in blankets of gold with bracelets and necklaces, earrings and crowns [Ezek. 16:11–13]. While it may appear lavish, the beauty of Christ and the finery of his Spirit are essential aspects of our life in God's Kingdom.

Fourthly, when a child is held by its mother it takes unimaginable delight. So it is with God's children for he keeps them very close and sits them on his knee [Is. 66:11].

Fifthly, a child usually resembles one of their parents. So much so that it is common to hear an onlooker declare, 'He's his father's son!' Those who have been born again come to share some of the features of their brother Jesus and in him, their heavenly Father [Gal. 4]. As with any proud father, God takes great pride and delight in his children. Others, who refuse to be part of this family, end up resembling those they cling to instead. Hence, those who love only the world bear the birthmark of this broken creation while those that love their heavenly Father radiate the realities of heaven.

Sixthly, having been gifted from God, good parents train their children in the habits and customs of the family house. So also, those that are born again live to the rhythmic wisdom of the church. Brought up, in God's house, they learn to cry, 'Father' and invite his response to direct their lives.

Seventhly, children rely on their father to meet their needs and fulfil their desires. If they want new shoes or fresh bread then they simply ask. So should the children of God. Do you want the kind of bread that satisfies every hunger? Well ask God for it. Do you want grace and mercy or strength to deny temptation? Go and tell him and when temptation comes, run home and pour out your heartfelt concerns and complaints to him. For this is what children do.…

As the child of a king, God's children must learn to live like the King. If they are risen with Christ, then their eyes and hearts and minds should focus on things above. The promises of the Father should be the subject of every family gathering. The whole clan should share love and determination to see the Father's will fulfilled and rest content with the implications of this sacrifice for every member. The family should live together lovingly, according to the guidelines laid down in his Word. They should affirm the image of God in others whenever they see it. Above all they should love one another over and over; serve one another again and again; heap good deed upon good deed for one day they will be joined together in heaven forever.

Lastly, disciples must learn to be obedient children of God, not shaped by what we once were but what we have become. Remember that God is your Father and let this one truth guide you so that you may one day look at up in him in peace.

More to think and pray …

1. Some of us forget to ask God for the things that we most desperately need and require. What is it that you most need from your heavenly Father? Take time to cry out for the things that you need today. You never know, your Father may hear and answer!

2. What do you want to do when you grow up? In what ways do you aspire to be more like your older brother Jesus and resemble your Father in heaven? How might you make steps towards this today?

3. How can we learn to live like a King? First, let us remind ourselves of the kind of kingship we find in Jesus. How can we imitate his own special servant-hearted brand of royalty?

Chapter Thirty-four

Praying Chess

IN THIS EXTRACT THERESA OF AVILA COMPARES PRAYER TO A GAME OF CHESS. IN PARTICULAR SHE IS INTERESTED IN THE DIFFERENCES BETWEEN 'MEDITATIVE PRAYER,' OR 'MEDITATION' AND 'CONTEMPLATIVE PRAYER,' OR 'CONTEMPLATION'. IN ESSENCE, THE FIRST IS THINKING ABOUT GOD, AND THE THINGS OF GOD, WHEREAS THE SECOND IS DIRECT EXPERIENCE OF GOD – SEEING OR 'CONTEMPLATING' GOD FACE TO FACE.

I hope you don't think I've written too much about this already – so far I've only set the board up! You asked me to tell you how to begin to pray. God did not lead me this way, my daughters, but this is all I know – indeed, I have hardly started in these elementary skills. But if you cannot set up the chessboard, you will never play chess well, and if you do not know how to give check, you will never reach checkmate. You will tell me off, of course, for talking about games we do not play in this house – we are forbidden to play them, indeed. Well, this will show you what sort of mother God has given you – she even knows about pointless things like this! Some people say that it is not wrong to play the game sometimes; it will not be wrong for us to play it like this, and if we play it often enough, we will quickly mate the Divine King! He will not escape, and He will not want to.

The queen is most dangerous to the king; all the other pieces support her. There is no queen who can beat this king so well as humility. Humility brought Him down from heaven into the virgin's womb, and humility allows us to pull Him into our souls easily. He will give much more humility to the one who has most, and little more to someone who has little. I don't know how humility can exist without love, or love without humility. These two virtues cannot exist unless we are removed from all created things.

You might ask, daughters, why I am telling you about virtues when you have more than enough books telling you about them, and when you want me to tell you about contemplative prayer. You see, if you had asked me about meditative prayer, I could have talked to you about that, and told you all to do it, even if you lack virtues like humility and love. This sort of prayer is the first step towards gaining these virtues, and Christian life depends on our beginning it. However far we have fallen, none of us should ignore such a blessing as this if God calls us to it. I've written about this in other places, and so have many others, who actually know what they are talking about. God knows that I don't!

But contemplative prayer, daughters – that's something completely different! We all make this mistake: if someone spends a few moments each day thinking about their sins, which anyone will do if they are really Christian, people immediately say this is true contemplation, and expect to find the virtues that a great contemplative will inevitably have. The person may even think that they have these virtues themselves – but this is a big mistake. At this point, we do not even know how to set up the pieces on the chessboard – we think that recognizing the pieces will be enough to win checkmate. But the King does not allow Himself to be taken except by one who surrenders completely to Him.

More to think and pray ...

1. Teresa argues that prayer depends on virtue; to what extent does this ring true in your experience of prayer?
2. Is the distinction between 'meditative' and 'contemplative' prayer something that you find helpful?
3. Chess was enormously popular in Spain in Teresa's day (chess players might be interested to know that she was a contemporary of Ruy Lopez, who gave his name to an opening still used today); can you think of ways of helpfully describing prayer in terms of football, or another pastime that you enjoy?

Chapter Thirty-five

Drink the Spirit

THIS EXTRACT IS TAKEN FROM A SERIES OF SERMONS PREACHED BY CATHERINE BOOTH ENTITLED *AGGRESSIVE CHRISTIANITY*. THIS PARTICULAR MESSAGE WAS GIVEN UNDER THE TITLE, 'FILLED WITH THE SPIRIT,' AND FEATURED TWO NEW TESTAMENT TEXTS . . .

While he was still with them, he said: Don't leave Jerusalem yet. Wait here for the Father to give you the Holy Spirit, just as I told you he has promised to do. John baptized with water, but in a few days you will be baptized with the Holy Spirit. [Acts 1:4–5, CEV]

Drink the Spirit of God. [Eph. 5:18]

God promises every disciple the gift of his Holy Spirit, whether young or old, strong or weak, experienced or inexperienced. God's generosity is not restricted to esteemed leaders, famed saints or celebrity Christians. In short, if we're prepared to put God first we'll experience his Spirit, whoever we are. As a result, nothing should threaten our loyalty to God; neither family nor friends; property nor possessions; work nor business; health nor leisure. In fact, if I cannot keep my life and be faithful to him then I must be willing to lose it for following Jesus is a sacrificial act. We start as we pick up his cross and continue to live with our heads on the block.

The promise of Pentecost is for every true believer. God wants us to have his Spirit. It's his gift to us at Christ's expense. He wants us to grab it so we too can live in apostolic power. So that we too can be totally transformed like Peter. Following his arrest and prior to Pentecost, Peter wouldn't publicly admit to knowing

Jesus. However, having been filled with the Spirit he followed Jesus courageously to his own execution.…

Notice how the first disciples had to wait for God's Spirit, just as Jesus had told them: 'Wait here for the Father to give you the Holy Spirit' [Acts 1:4]. Who did they expect? What were they thinking? How did they feel as they waited? They surely would have talked over all they had seen; the glorious and divine events of Christ's resurrection; the unforgettable adventures from three years on the road; the changes Jesus had made in their own lives; the times they had doubted; the disappointment of losing him to heaven so soon after their last reunion; the things that might have been if he had only stayed a little longer. And how many were their regrets? If only the penny had dropped sooner. If only they had seen what now seemed obvious. If only they had asked, learned, grasped and grabbed more of him while they could.

As I reflect on that scene, I can imagine a heartbroken Peter throwing himself face down in humiliation. Thomas must have felt similarly? But these two were not alone; think of the others shamefully reminiscing about the events that followed Jesus' betrayal. After all, where were they during Jesus' detention, trial, torture and execution? It is almost impossible for us to imagine the desperation with which the disciples waited in that upper room.

But here's the point: stooping low is the first and indispensable condition for receiving the Holy Spirit. We must acknowledge our past, our impurity, our disobedience and ingratitude. We shouldn't shy away from the worst of ourselves. We should remember the moments when we chose to betray or ignore him. We should consider our unfaithfulness, the times when we have shrunk from the cross and stayed loyal to the world. If we want to be filled with the Spirit, we must be willing to know and confess the worst of ourselves. We must say, 'Lord, I have sunk so low that only you can lift me up so please fill unholy me with your Holy Spirit.' It is only after we empty ourselves that God can fill us up. If we're full of ourselves then we have no need of God. If we think we can get by without him, he'll simply stand by and watch us try to prove it. But if we want his Holy Spirit we must first realize how helpless and weak we are.…

The disciples also waited in earnest and eager expectation for Pentecost. There were, after all, about 120 of them there waiting. And while they no doubt told stories of days gone by, of Jesus' life, death and resurrection they surely also looked forward to the future. For Jesus had told them that they would go to Jerusalem – the city where he had met his end – and proclaim the beginning of his new Kingdom. From there on they would witness the global domination of the gospel of peace. And yet, as they waited there, knowing what Jesus had planned for them, they must have trembled at how terribly ill equipped they were for the task. Poor Peter, and Thomas, and John, and Mary and the rest of the women, how must they have felt? I'm sure they must have prayed, 'Lord, pour out your Spirit. We need it. We want it. We're ready and waiting.'

Any of us who lives with a calling or vocation, a sense of knowing what God wants us to do and how he wants us to live, understands the fear which Jesus' disciples shared before Pentecost. However, like them, we can and must trust him for his promised power. After all, we won't be able to begin our journey until that power arrives from on high. Having taken possession of his power God takes possession of us. From here on we are moved, inspired, energized and empowered by the indwelling of his Spirit....

Lastly, the disciples waited out of obedience. For once, they did what Jesus asked.... In days gone by they had grown up, become stronger in their faith and so trusted Jesus' word like never before....

While disobedient faith walks away empty, obedient faith receives what it's waiting for. If the Lord has told you to wait and you move on too quickly, you'll never receive what you're waiting for and never gain what he's giving. On the other hand, obedient faith receives all that God has promised and leads directly to his Kingdom. If you wish to see that destination then do as God asks you, sacrifice when he calls you and go where he leads you for he has reserved the greatest of gifts for those disciples who serve him with all they have; disciples who have an obedient faith.

More to think and pray ...

1. Are you ready and waiting? Take time to wait on God's Spirit. Set aside some quality time to wait for God to encourage, challenge or transform you.
2. How needy are you? How desperate are you to encounter and be filled with God's Spirit. What areas of your life are most in need of his presence and power? Using one of the oldest prayers of the church pray, 'Veni Sancti Spiritus' (Come Holy Spirit), invite God's Spirit in to your greatest area of need.
3. How obedient are you? Consider how ready, willing and available you are to follow Jesus' call today. Where is he asking you to go? What is he asking you to do? How willing are you to sacrifice? Be encouraged! The Spirit's power often takes hold of us when we prove willing to grapple with these questions.

The Bible

'But whoso hath this world's good, and seeth his brother have need, and shutteth up his bowels of compassion from him, how dwelleth the love of God in him?'

1 John 3:17

Jacob Bronowski (1908–74)

'The world can only be grasped by action, not by contemplation ... The hand is the cutting edge of the mind.'

The Ascent of Man (1973), ch. 3

Chapter Thirty-six

The Work of the Spirit

THESE POEMS ARE TAKEN FROM *THE TEMPLE*,
BY GEORGE HERBERT.

Whitsunday

Listen sweet Dove unto my song,
And spread thy golden wings in me;
Hatching my tender heart so long,
Till it get wing, and fly away with thee.

Where is that fire which once descended
On thy Apostles? Thou didst then
Keep open house, richly attended,
Feasting all comers by twelve chosen men.

Such glorious gifts thou didst bestow,
That the earth did like a heaven appear;
The stars were coming down to know
If they might mend their wages, and serve here.

The sun, which once did shine alone,
Hung down his head, and wished for night,
When he beheld twelve suns for one
Going about the world, and giving light.

But since those pipes of gold, which brought
That cordial water to our ground,
Were cut and martyred by the fault
Of those, who did themselves through their side wound,

Thou shuts the door, and keeps within;
Scarce a good joy creeps through the chink:
And if the braves of conquering sin
Did not excite thee, we should wholly sink.

Lord, though we change, thou art the same;
The same sweet God of love and light:
Restore this day, for thy great name,
Unto his ancient and miraculous right.

Employment

IF as a flower doth spread and die,
Thou wouldst extend me to some good,
Before I were by frost's extremity
                    Nipped in the bud;

The sweetness and the praise were thine;
But the extension and the room,
Which in thy garland I should fill, were mine
                    At thy great doom.

For as thou dost impart thy grace,
The greater shall our glory be.
The measure of our joys is in this place,
                    The stuff with thee.

Let me not languish then, and spend
A life as barren to thy praise,
As is the dust, to which that life doth tend,
                    But with delays.

All things are busy; only I
Neither bring honey with the bees,
Nor flowers to make that, nor the husbandry
                    To water these.

I am no link of thy great chain,
But all my company is a weed.
Lord place me in thy consort; give one strain
                    To my poor reed.

Trinity Sunday

Lord, who hast formed me out of mud,
  And hast redeemed me through thy blood,
  And sanctified me to do good;

Purge all my sins done heretofore:
  For I confess my heavy score,
  And I will strive to sin no more.

Enrich my heart, mouth, hands in me,
  With faith, with hope, with charity;
  That I may run, rise, rest with thee.

More to think and pray ...

1. Which of the biblical images for the Holy Spirit that Herbert uses do you find most puzzling? What can you learn from it?
2. 'Lord, though we change, thou art the same.' Herbert is suggesting that the difference between the New Testament experience of the Holy Spirit and ours is a change in us, not in what God is doing. Do you think he is right?
3. The two latter poems suggest that the chief work of human beings is giving God praise. What one thing could you do to make this more of a reality in your life?

Chapter Thirty-seven

Approaching God

THIS EXTRACT HAS BEEN TAKEN FROM THE
'CONVERSATIONS OF BROTHER LAWRENCE'.

Brother Lawrence spoke to me eagerly and passionately about the way he approached God – I've said some of this already.

He said the heart of it all was one moment of giving up completely everything – everything – that we feel does not lead us to God. After this, we can get used to just talking to God constantly. There is no mystery or technique about this – it's simple. The only thing we need to do is recognize that God is intimately present with us every moment, and speak to him all the time – to ask help from Him, to know what He wants us to do when it is not clear, and to do well when it is clear what He wants us to do. We should dedicate our tasks to Him before we do them, and thank Him when we are finished.

During this constant conversation with God we also spend our time in endlessly praising God, adoring and loving Him because He is so good to us and so perfect in Himself.

We should ask for God's help with complete confidence, not considering our own weaknesses, but pointing to the infinite worth of our Lord Jesus. God never fails to offer us help in everything. Brother Lawrence said he was always aware of this, unless he had been distracted from his awareness of God's presence, or forgotten to ask God's help.

Brother Lawrence said that when we were confused or doubting, God would always give us understanding – if our only desire was to please Him.

He said that we become holy not through changing the things that we do, but by doing for God the things we normally do for ourselves. It is sad to see how many people devote themselves only to doing certain things, which they do badly because of their selfishness, and so confuse means and ends.

He had found that the best way of coming to God was living out our ordinary lives without trying to impress other people. Instead we should do all the things we have to do only out of love for God.

He said it was foolish to think that our prayer times should be different from other times. We should come close to God by business in times of business, as much as by prayer in times of prayer.

His prayer, he said, was simply an awareness of the presence of God. When he was praying, he forgot everything, because he was overwhelmed by a sense of God's love. When the set hours of prayer in the monastery were over, it was no different: he continued to praise God, and to worship Him with all his strength. Because of this, his life was full of constant joy – but he hoped that God might allow him to suffer some things when he was stronger.

He said we ought to put our trust in God, completely and at once. We ought to give ourselves up to Him. God will not mislead us.

Also, we ought not to get tired of doing little things out of love for God. God does not care about the size of the task; he cares about how much love is involved. We should not be surprised if we fail regularly at the start, but in the end it will become a habit, and without thinking we will start to live in a way that will bring us great joy.

The only things that will bring us into God's will are faith, hope and love. Nothing else matters, unless we can use it as a bridge, and run over it quickly, to get to our one end of confidence and love.

Everything is possible for someone who believes; it is easier for someone who hopes, and easier still for someone who loves. Everything is easy if we keep living out these three virtues.

The goal we ought to set ourselves for this life is to become the most perfect worshippers of God that we can. That is what we hope to be for all eternity, after all!

Brother Lawrence added that when we set out on our spiritual journey we should examine ourselves, search out our most basic desires and motivations. We will find that we are not worthy of any respect, not even worthy of the title 'Christian,' the victims of all sorts of unhappiness and endless circumstances that trouble us, and damage our health, physically, mentally and spiritually. We will discover that we are people who God must humble by many pains and much labour – working on ourselves, as well as working in the world. After uncovering all this, why should we be surprised by the troubles and temptations, the opposition and contradiction, we find from other people? We should put up with them, bear them as long as God pleases – these things will do us good!

He ended by telling me this: the higher we aim, the more dependent on divine grace we will be.

More to think and pray ...

1. The passage above flows from a conversation between friends into moments of praise and worship. How might we more naturally introduce moments of prayer into the every day stuff of life?

2. Lawrence reminds us that our spiritual life, work and mission are all aspects of our worship. Take time at the beginning of each day to commit your schedule to God as an act of worship and mission.

Chapter Thirty-eight

Faith in the Desert

THIS EXTRACT WAS TAKEN FROM THE WRITINGS OF
THE DESERT FATHERS.

One Father had two brothers for neighbours, one a foreigner, and
the other local. The foreigner was a little lax, and the local monk
was very devout. One day, the foreigner died. The Father had the
gift of vision, and he saw many angels escorting his soul. When
he was at the gates of heaven, there was a question over him, and
a voice from on high said 'Clearly, he was a little lax, but for the
sake of his pilgrimage, let him in.'

A little later, the local brother died, and all his family had come.
The Father saw no angels anywhere. He was astonished, and
threw himself on his face before God. He said 'How come that
foreigner, who was lax, received such glory, whereas this one, who
was devout, received nothing?'

And a voice came, and it said to him 'This devout monk, on the
point of death, opened his eyes and saw his family crying, and
he was comforted; but the foreigner, although he was lax, saw
no-one who loved him, and so he wept in sorrow. And so God
has comforted him.'

✛

A Father said, 'If a monk knows a place where he could grow, but
where he would struggle to get the things he needs for life, and
does not go there for that reason – that monk does not believe
that God exists!'

✛

A brother asked a Father 'What thing is so good that I may do it and live through it?' The Father said 'Only God knows what is good – but I have heard that one of the Fathers questioned the great Abbot Nistero, the friend of Antony himself, and said "What good work shall I do?" Nistero answered "All works are not equal. We read that Abraham was hospitable, and God was with him. Elijah loved peace, and God was with him. David was humble, and God was with him. So, do what your heart desires in following God.'

✛

Mother Syncletica said, 'It is painful, and hard work, to come to God at the beginning. When we have come to God, however, our joy will be beyond words. It is like lighting a fire: first you get a face full of smoke, and the smoke makes you weep, but then the fire burns. (It is said in Scripture, 'Our God is a consuming fire' [Heb. 12:29].) We have to kindle the divine fire in us with struggle, and with tears.

✛

Once the holy Epiphanius [Bishop of Cyprus] sent a message to the Abbot Hilarion, saying 'Come and let me see you before I die.' When they met, they were eating together, and a chicken dish was brought to them. The bishop took it, and gave it to Hilarion. The Father said to him, 'Forgive me, but from the day I became a monk, I have been vegetarian.' Then the bishop said, 'Since I have been a bishop, I have let no-one go to sleep if they had anything against me, and I have not gone to sleep with anything against anyone.' The Father said to him, 'I am sorry – your rule of life is better than mine.'

More to think and pray ...

1. Whose rule of life is better than yours? Think of a few people who you admire and aspire to be like. What is it about their character and behaviour that impresses you? How might you learn from them?
2. Don't let the sun go down on anger. Rather than continue another day in bitterness or resentment against another brother or sister make a plan to restore and be reconciled as soon as possible.
3. Pray that God will use your own life story to communicate his good news to the world.

Samuel Butler

'They would have been equally horrified at hearing the Christian religion doubted, and at seeing it practised.'

The Way of All Flesh

Chapter Thirty-nine

Turned Pillows

THE FOLLOWING POEMS BY MARIANNE FARNINGHAM
ENTITLED, 'TURNED PILLOWS' AND 'WHO MEETS THE
NEED' WERE INSPIRED RESPECTIVELY BY A LINE IN A
LETTER AND DR BARNARDO'S FAMOUS LAST WORDS.

'it is such a comfort to her to have her pillow turned; it seems to soothe and refresh her. she told me she wished someone would write a poem on turned pillows; so wondered if you would.' – a letter

Turned Pillows

I READ the words with sympathy:
　　But still my own heart sometimes asks,
Why does God let such suffering be?
　　Why set His own such fearful tasks?
Yet faith has here her victories won, –
'The Lord is good: His will be done.'

I have not seen this tired, hot head,
　　The weary eyes that speak of pain,
The restless tossing on the bed,
　　The nights whose tedious hours remain,
But much of this we all have seen,
And I can read the lines between.

My heart aches for you, dear unknown;
　　Yet God some compensation sends:
He does not leave His child alone,
　　Love looks through eyes of many friends,

And when pain's fever aches and burns,
Love's tender hands the pillow turns.
It is a little thing to do,
        And yet it is a prophecy;
Christ's kind hand oft is laid on you,
        That Love's sweet vision you may see:
And you will know the deep, cool rest
Of those who sleep on Jesus' breast.

The hours of pain need pillows turned,
        But soon another day will break,
When God has taught and you have learned
        What He can do for Love's dear sake.
You will forget each painful thing
When your glad eyes have seen the King.

(AMONG THE LAST WORDS UTTERED BY DR BARNARDO WERE THESE:
'THE CHILDREN WILL NEED ME MORE THAN EVER THIS WINTER.')

Who Meets the Need?

The strong heart had grown weaker,
        Brave eyes through pain were dim,
He thought of his large family –
        But the Father thought of him:
He deemed the children needed him,
        God knew *he* needed rest,
And gave him sudden quietness
        And the joy of ended quest.

Ah! England has her patriots
        Who for her glory fight:
Barnardo rescued her from shame,
        And gave her love and light;
A greater patriot than them all,
        A holier war he fought;
And what would England be today,
        But for Barnardo's thought?

Full fifty thousand boys and girls
 Untaught, unsaved, he won:
Think, if he had not rescued them
 What evils had they done!
He loved them into being good,
 He found them home and friends;
His trophies they, prepared, equipped
 For lives of noblest ends.

It will take many brave, strong souls
 To fill Barnardo's place!
But he awoke men's pity
 And taught them acts of grace:
And a thousand workers do his work,
 Ten thousand pray his prayers –
The waifs are no more desolate
 For every Christian cares.

More to think and pray ...

1. What avenues of service and ministry offer you the opportunity to bring Christ's goodness into the lives of others? How might your life impact those who have given up believing in God's presence or goodness?
2. What are the issues that have hold of your heart in your own community? How might you respond to these and rally others to be involved in bringing hope?
3. As part of your discipleship, make a plan to meet another's need this week and rest assured that in carrying this out Christ will join you along the way.

Chapter Forty

Real Faith in the Real World

THIS EXTRACT IS TAKEN FROM A SERMON ORIGINALLY ENTITLED 'THE WORLD'S NEED', PREACHED BY CATHERINE BOOTH IN THE WEST END OF LONDON IN THE SUMMER OF 1880. THE MESSAGE WAS THE NINTH IN A SERIES OF TEN SERMONS WHICH WERE LATER PUBLISHED UNDER THE TITLE *AGGRESSIVE CHRISTIANITY*. HER TEXT WAS LUKE 14:23.

The master said, 'Then go to the country roads. Whoever you find, drag them in. I want my house full! Let me tell you, not one of those originally invited is going to get so much as a bite at my dinner party.' [Lk. 14:23, *The Message*]

While we have numerous texts teaching the same truth, the main thrust of God's Word is more particular and powerful than any individual sentence or verse. The most uninspired Bible reader can see that God's light shines far and wide; his love, extensive and his grace, expansive. In dishing out his good news, God commissions us to pass it on. Hence real Christianity is aggressive Christianity. True faith is intentional and infectious, insistent and industrious. Jesus says it all in a parable. Before we finish reading or hearing the tale it has become obvious that we too must tell God's story far and wide.

The first Christians took up Christ's challenge wonderfully. To us, they look almost carefree, cheerfully giving up everything, every care and concern, allegiance and anxiety to follow Jesus and share him with others. Take Paul, he gladly gave up all he had to travel, work, pray, weep, suffer, bleed and eventually die to shout aloud the good news. The Early Church, though scattered by persecution, continued to preach Christ crucified throughout the ancient world. Subsequent generations, so church history teaches, travelled to the very ends of the earth to make disciples and often paid a great price. Whether in the finest palace or most fetid slum, nothing prevented these followers of Jesus going about their beautiful business. They could not be kept out and neither would they get out. They would not put up or shut up! Never a day out of season, they kept watch both day and night, loving, preaching and winning men, women and children for Christ's kingdom. Though their enemies tried they would not hide. What's more, the irrepressible Spirit and joy of their risen Lord spilt onto every place and person they encountered.

As God's people we have travelled a long way. So much so that I become ever more mystified by how Christians misread his book! They don't seem to get it. For some, a right reading of the text seems to require an angelic visitation and even then this may not work. You see, the maxim – no matter how well worn – simply isn't true. The New Testament makes it alarmingly clear that we *are* our brother's keeper. In short, God holds us responsible for the salvation of others.

Oh! I wish I could get this through to you. The fact is that Jesus has no other work force. We are it. The rest of the world, all those who are yet to meet our wonderful saviour and friend, have nobody else to make the introduction. If *we* do not reach them with his loving kindness; if *we* don't hatch a rescue plan to save them from their lives; if *we* do not by the Holy Spirit tie Satan's hands and snatch them free from the brink of death who else will? Alarmingly, the answer is no one.

Now, my friends, we are called by the Spirit to this work. Obey the call. Do it! Never mind if it kills you. Do it! Know that it's better to die than live in disobedience. Do it! Don't make excuses or let yourself off too easily. Do it! Don't stop for fear of the consequences. Do it! God will take care of the consequences and if these cause you to suffer, be consoled that this is because you have obeyed the Spirit.

Think how the world would be different if all Christ's disciples obeyed him? Learn to recognize the sound of his voice, pray that you will discern his slightest urge. Be sure that your aspirations are born of God and not your own agenda. Check that these promptings are not the work of Satan who will always try to deceive you. Above all, rest assured that it is the Spirit of God that presses you to seek and save the lost. Will you hear? Will you obey? Will you stop justifying your inaction? Will you risk? Will you sacrifice? Will you do it! If you do, then you will see him, hear and know him more and more.

More to think and pray ...

1. How intentional are you about your faith? How does what you know and what you are learning from Christ inform your day-to-day life and decision-making?

2. How conscious are you of God's desire and plan to use you in telling his story to others? How might you find new and creative ways of communicating the gospel to those who haven't yet heard the good news? With whom can you share Jesus' good news today in an explicit way?

3. How live is the conversation between Jesus and yourself? How do you best hear his voice and how often are you aware of it? How might you practise your listening skills in days and weeks to come?

Benjamin Disraeli (1st Earl of Beaconsfield) (1804–81)

British Conservative politician and novelist;
Prime Minister, 1868, 1874–80

'Experience is the child of Thought, and Thought is the child of Action. We cannot learn men from books.'

Vivian Grey (1826) bk. 6, ch. 7

Biographies and Bibliographies of Featured Writers

The 'Desert Fathers' (c. 200–c. 400 CE)

The original desert hermits of Egypt were Christians who had fled to the less habitable regions surrounding the main towns in order to escape persecution under the Roman Emperor Diocletian at the beginning of the third century. Despite the 'legalization' of Christianity by Constantine in 313, a small number of young men, attracted by the solitude of the desert, chose to stay, believing that the stark reality of desert life provided an ideal training ground for a much more self-disciplined and deliberate pursuit of God's call. As these desert-dwellers developed a reputation for holiness and wisdom, others were attracted from further afield. Later monks, such as Antony the Great and Pachomius, developed the desert life from what was essentially a very individual spiritual programme into a more structured and community-centred approach, introducing practices such as common prayer and meals, which would eventually develop into Christian monasticism. The wisdom of the Desert Fathers is usually found in the forms of short, pithy sayings and stories, many of which are anonymous.

Key Works: collections of the sayings of the desert fathers began to circulate very early on in several different languages (we have translated from the Greek collections in most cases). Several manuscripts of different collections have survived, and now extracts from them may be found published under many different titles. Most of them, however, contain the sub-title 'The Sayings/Wisdom/Spirituality of the Desert Fathers'.

St Benedict of Nursia (c. 480–c. 547)

Benedict was born in Nursia (in the Umbria region of Italy), the son of a Roman noble. Dating his life is difficult, as our only source for the monk's life – Pope Gregory I's four-volume *Dialogues*, written in 593 – doesn't give such details, although we can estimate that he moved away from Rome in his twenties, settling down in Enfide in the Simbruini mountains, and at some point met the monk Romanus, on whose advice he then became a hermit and lived for three years in a cave. This period, during which Benedict matured in mind and character, was the beginning of a lifetime spent founding twelve communities for monks and developing his 'Holy Rule', a sort of instruction manual for Christian living that was so influential to Western Christendom that Benedict is often referred to as 'the founder of Western Christian monasticism'.

Key Works: The Holy Rule of St Benedict.

Mother Julian of Norwich (c. 1342–c. 1416)

Little is known about this English mystic, although reliable tradition links her with St Julian's church in Norwich, near which she practised a life of meditation and prayer in solitude. Her writings reveal that she was an intensely passionate individual, even asking God in her youth for a 'gift' of a life-threatening bodily sickness at the age of 30, so that she might worship God more gratefully if she recovered from it, or be with him if she did not. She did become sick as she had prayed, and near the end of this period received sixteen intense visions, or revelations, of the sufferings of the Christ and the Trinity. Her reflections on these visions over the next twenty years, which centred on God's love rather than his judgement, formed the basis of her best known work, *Revelations of Divine Love*.

Key Works: The Sixteen Revelations of Divine Love.

Thomas À Kempis (1380–1471)

Thomas Hammercken was born in the town of Kempen in Germany (hence, à Kempis), amid threats of constant war, bouts of the Black Plague and the unsettlement of the Great Schism. He was educated in a Dutch school run by 'The Brothers of the Common Life', monks devoted to simplicity, prayer and oneness with God who had such a positive influence on the young Thomas that he decided to live his life according to the same ideals. At the age of 19 he moved into the monastery of Mount St Agnes, where he spent his time in prayer, study, copying manuscripts, teaching novices, offering Mass and hearing the confession of visitors to the monastery church, and stayed there until his death 72 years later. During this time he also wrote the classic text on spiritual life, *The Imitation of Christ*.

Key Works: The Imitation of Christ. *Thomas wrote many other works, but they have not enjoyed the wide circulation of the* Imitation, *and often are only accessible in nineteenth-century Latin editions.*

St Teresa of Ávila (1515–82)

Teresa de Cepeda y Ahumada was born in Ávila, Spain, the daughter of a strict Toledo merchant and his second wife, and as a young child showed evidence of a deeply religious nature, no doubt influenced by her pious Catholic upbringing. At 15, her mother died, causing her to be entrusted shortly afterwards to the care of Augustinian nuns. She had natural charisma and found it easy to make friends – things she felt terribly guilty about, possibly as a result of her father's exacting standards. Shortly after joining the Carmelite order aged 20, she became sick with malaria, which left her legs paralysed and her body in severe pain over a three-year period, and then experienced a vision of 'the sorely wounded Christ' which deeply affected her, and inspired her to reform her order. At age 43 she decided to establish a new order recommitting to the values of poverty and simplicity, but rather than stress the way of rigid self denial she instead stressed the need to experience God's love.

Key Works: The Life of Teresa of Jesus, The Interior Castle, The Way of Perfection.

George Herbert (1593–1633)

George Herbert was born in Montgomery, in Wales. His family was influential and artistic (his mother knew the poet John Donne), and he enjoyed academic success, leading to appointments at Cambridge University, and political patronage, then to a seat in parliament and the King's favour. Circumstances turned against him, and he moved to be vicar of Bemerton, a rural parish in Wiltshire. Just three years later, he died of TB. On his deathbed, he gave a manuscript of poems to a friend, asking him to publish them if they were of any worth. These poems have secured Herbert a lasting place in English literature, and among Christian devotional writers.

Key Works: The Temple *(collected poems)*; The Country Parson, or, A Priest in the Temple *(pastoral advice)*.

Brother Lawrence (c. 1614–91)

Beginning life as Nicholas Herman and born to peasant parents in Lorraine, France, his poverty led him to joining the army, where he was at least guaranteed meals. After a subsequent stint as a valet, at 24 he joined the Discalced (shoeless) Carmelite Prior in Paris as a lay brother – not having the education to become a cleric – and took the religious name 'Lawrence of the Resurrection'. He was assigned to the monastery kitchen where, amid the tedium of his chores, he developed his rule of spirituality and work, which saw every piece of 'common business' as an opportunity to practise the presence of God. By 1666, Brother Lawrence's unusual yet profound wisdom had captured the attention of the Cardinal de Noailles, who sent his envoy and investigator Abbé de Beaufort. Most of our knowledge of Brother Lawrence and his wisdom are a result of four interviews that took place between the two men.

Key Works: The Practice of the Presence of God *(a collection of Br Lawrence's own writings, and of reports of conversations with him).*

John Bunyan (1628–88)

Bunyan, a poor travelling tinker like his father, was married at 21 to a woman who was also so poor she only brought two Puritan books as a dowry. These two books proved to be the starting point for his conversion, motivating him to give up recreations such as dancing and bell ringing and instead to attend church. Before long, Bunyan was a popular lay preacher in the Separatist Church, drawing crowds from all around and consequently being imprisoned for preaching without a licence when Charles II, the head of the Church of England, was restored to the throne in 1661. His twelve years of incarceration afforded him the time to write several books, the most well known being the allegorical *The Pilgrim's Progress*, which became an instant success among all social classes. Upon his release and subsequent licensing as a Congregational minister, he pastored a church in Bedford, dying at the age of 59, having become ill riding through heavy rain to reconcile a father and son.

Key Works: Christian Behaviour, The Holy City, Grace Abounding for the Chief of Sinners *(an autobiography),* The Pilgrim's Progress.

John Wesley (1703–91)

John Wesley was born in Epworth, near Lincoln, the fifteenth of nineteen children, all of whom were educated by their parents. During his life and ministry (initially as an Anglican minister) he was based in various places, which were all instrumental in the development of his beliefs and practices. In Oxford, where he went to university, he was part of a 'holy club' formed by his younger brother Charles, which was the melting point for Methodism. He spent three years as a missionary and pastor in Savannah, Georgia, and although this time was marred by an unhappy relationship with a woman, it is where he first met with the Moravians and the Arminian movement in general, which would heavily influence his theological ideas. Bristol was where Wesley first preached in the open air, with much reticence but under the urging of his friend George Whitefield, the evangelist. He travelled widely, mostly by horse, had a very simple, methodical but hardworking lifestyle, and was a logical thinker, as is evident in his sermons and other writings.

Key Texts: Wesley's writings were voluminous. Many of them, particularly collections of his sermons, are available in various published formats.

Catherine Booth (1829–90)

Born in Ashbourne, Derbyshire and raised in the typically pious and sheltered world of small-town Victorian England, Catherine Mumford had a strong Christian upbringing. Forced to remain in bed for months at a time as a result of a spinal curvature, the young Catherine read voraciously, particularly the works of Finney and Wesley, and by the age of 12 had read the whole Bible eight times. Marrying the Methodist minister William Booth in 1855, she became very active in the work of her husband's church, and grew convinced that God had called her to a speaking ministry despite this being unheard of among women in her day. In 1865, the two started the work of The Christian Mission, with William preaching to the poor and Catherine speaking to the wealthy to raise essential funds for their ministry, which eventually became known as The Salvation Army. She was behind many of the changes in the new organization, contributing particularly to the Army's ideas on doctrine and practice.

Key Texts: Aggressive Christianity.

Marianne Farningham (1834–1909)

Marianne Farningham is the pseudonym of the writer and poet Mary Anne Hearn, who was born in the Kentish town of Farningham but was known as 'Polly' to her family and friends. Although her schooling was cut short by the death of her mother, which meant that instead she was doing all the housework and looking after her three siblings at the age of 12, for most of her life she taught alongside her writing in British schools in Bristol, Gravesend and Northampton. Through her teaching she realized that she had a gift in and a liking for talking to large groups, and as she became increasingly popular through her weekly contributions to *The Christian World* and *The Sunday School Times*, she gained increasing opportunity to travel, which she relished.

Key Texts: Lays and Lyrics of the Blessed Life, Poems, A Working Woman's Life.